Kenji Ito ⁰/₀ First Pres. X ch.
Berkeley

Jap

PhD student at Cal. in Oriental languages. One
head of Navigator work in Japan. Raised Buddhist —
became a Chr. by reading "Father forgive them".
"What kind of man could say that?".

A Dr. of Music from Univ of Oregon said that he
comes from Lapland, Calif which is near
Cucamonga. A girl called, what she that
was a record shop, but which instead was a
Plumbers office. "Hello" "Do you have 10 toes
& 10 fingers in Wyoming?" A pause. Then, "I'm
sorry lady, could you give me that again." She
repeats.

He said; "No but I have 10 kids; one
wife in Cucamonga" She said "Is that a
record"; "Well - he said - we're ahead of
than our neighbors". so far we're ahead of

FISHERS OF MEN

By

WILLIAM BARCLAY, D.D.

LONDON : EPWORTH PRESS

© WILLIAM BARCLAY 1966

FIRST PUBLISHED IN 1966
by THE EPWORTH PRESS

Book Steward
FRANK H. CUMBERS

SET IN MONOTYPE PLANTIN AND PRINTED IN
GREAT BRITAIN BY THE CAMELOT PRESS LTD
LONDON AND SOUTHAMPTON

Contents

Seven of the chapters forming this book were originally independent lectures. Chapter 1 is the eleventh Joseph Smith Memorial Lecture, which was delivered in the George Cadbury Hall, Selly Oak, Birmingham, on 1st October 1960; chapters 2, 3, 4 and 5 were delivered to the British Secretaries' Association of the YMCA; chapter 6 was delivered to the Lay Preachers of the Congregational Union of England and Wales, and chapter 7 to the Religious Booksellers Group of the Booksellers Association. Chapter 8 is reprinted from the *Expository Times*.

I

Fishers of Men

THERE can be nothing more clear and more unmistakable than *the commission of the evangelist of Jesus Christ*. 'Follow me,' said Jesus to his first disciples, 'and I will make you become fishers of men' (Mark 1¹⁷; Matthew 4¹⁹). 'The harvest is plentiful,' he said, 'but the labourers are few; pray therefore the Lord of the harvest to send out labourers into his harvest' (Matthew 9³⁷, ³⁸; Luke 10²) 'Go! Preach!' the imperatives of Jesus Christ ring out with their unmistakable challenge to His Church (Matthew 10⁵⁻⁷; Luke 9²). Beyond a doubt the Christian has his marching orders.

Equally clear and unmistakable is *the sphere in which this commission is to be carried out*. The sphere is nothing less than the whole wide world, and the aim is nothing less than a world for Christ. 'Go, therefore,' comes the command, 'and make disciples of all nations' (Matthew 28¹⁹). 'Go into all the world and preach the gospel to the whole creation' (Mark 16¹⁵). It was because God so loved the world that He sent his Son (John 3¹⁶). The dream is the dream of a world in which every knee shall bow and every tongue confess that Jesus Christ is Lord (Philippians 2¹¹).

No one can read the New Testament without being confronted with the *allness* of the Christian message. When Paul describes his work, he describes himself as warning *every man*, and teaching *every man*, that we may present *every man* mature in Christ (Colossians 1²⁸). The Pastoral Epistles speak of God who desires *all men* to be saved and to come to a knowledge of the truth, and speak of Christ Jesus who gave Himself a ransom for *all* (I Timothy 2⁴, ⁵). In the Fourth Gospel Jesus says: 'I, when I am lifted up from the earth, will draw *all men* to myself' (John 12³²). Even if the day of separation is to come, the dragnet in the first instance gathers in things of every kind (Matthew 13⁴⁷). When the invited guests refuse the invitation to the marriage feast, the servants of the king must go out to the highways and the byways and gather in all who can be found. 'Still there is room,' is the report of the servant (Matthew 22¹⁻¹⁴; Luke 14¹⁶⁻²⁴). In the account of the dimensions of the Holy City, the new Jerusalem, we are told that each side of the city measures 12,000 stades. A stade was very nearly a furlong, so that is to say that each side of the city is 1,500 miles long. That is to say the total area of the city is 2,250,000 square miles! (Revelation 21¹⁶). The room within the Holy City is limitless in its extent.

Jesus Christ cannot be satisfied with less than the world. William Temple said: 'If the gospel is true for any man anywhere, it is true for all men everywhere.' And he also said: 'The Church exists for those who are not yet members of it.' The area of the Christian commission is nothing smaller than the world. There is no man, woman or child whom God does not want. During the days of the war there was an inevitable but a terrible word, the word *expendable*. In any military operation so many men were reckoned expendable; they could be killed, they could be eliminated, without the success of the operation failing or being jeopardized. In the operation of God there is no such thing as a human being who is expendable. Paul Tournier in *A Doctor's Casebook in the Light of the Bible* tells of a patient of his who was the youngest daughter of a large family, a family which the father found it very difficult to support. One day she heard him mutter despairingly, referring to herself: 'We could well have done without that one!' There is no one whom God can do without. The old story of Muretus enshrines a great truth. Muretus was a wandering scholar, very learned and very poor. In his wanderings he fell ill and he was taken to the place where the destitute were kept. They did not know that he was a scholar and that he understood the scholar's Latin. The doctors were discussing his case in Latin. They were saying that he was a poor creature of value to no one, and that it was hopeless and unnecessary to expend care and money on attention to such a worthless one. Muretus looked up and answered in their own Latin: 'Call no man worthless for whom Christ died.'

The sphere of the Christian commission is clear and un-mistakable; the sphere is the world. The missionary task of the Church at home and abroad is not an optional extra; it is a primary and essential obligation.

The commission of the Christian and the sphere in which that commission operates are both clear and unmistakable; and just as clear and unmistakable is *the function of the evangelist. The function of every Christian is to be a part of the body of Christ.*

One of the great New Testament pictures of the Church is the picture of the Church as the Body of Christ. 'You are the body of Christ,' wrote Paul to the Corinthians, 'and individually members of it' (I Corinthians 12²⁷). 'He is the head of the body, the church,' he writes to the Colossians (Colossians 1¹⁸). 'The church', he writes, 'which is his body' (Ephesians 1²³).

The picture here is unmistakable. The Church is to be the body through which Jesus Christ acts and works. Jesus is now no longer in this world in the body, though He is here powerfully in the Spirit. But that means that, if Jesus Christ wants something done, He must find a man or a woman through whom He can act. Here, for instance, is a child. Jesus Christ wants that child taught. Nothing on earth can teach that child unless a man or a woman is prepared to undertake the task—for Christ. The Church has to be the body of Christ in the most literal sense that in the Church Jesus Christ must find lips to speak for Him, hands to do His work, feet to run upon His errands. We often speak of the might and the majesty and the power of God, but there is a sense in which in all reverence we can do no other than think and speak of the helplessness of God, for unless God can find human hearts and hands through which His work may be done that work cannot be done.

There are two passages in Paul in which this idea comes out most distinctly. The first is Ephesians 1[23]. There Paul speaks of the Church as his body, 'the fulness of him who fills all in all'. The word for *fulness* is *plērōma*. What does this word *plērōma* mean? There are in Greek two very significant uses of this word. First, it can and does mean a ship's crew. Xenophon (*Hellenica* 1.6.16) explains the exceptional speed of a galley by saying that to man it, 'the best oarsmen had been picked out of a great many crews', and the word for *crews* is *plērōmata*. Second, Aristotle in the *Politics* (4.3.12; 1291a) tells how Socrates laid down the essential elements in any city, the basic elements out of which the life of any city must be constructed. 'Socrates says that the most necessary elements of which a state is composed are four, and he specifies these as a weaver, a farmer, a shoemaker, and a builder; and then again he adds, on the ground that these are not self-sufficient, a coppersmith, and the people to look after the necessary livestock, and in addition a merchant and a retail trader. These elements together constitute *the full complement* of his first city.' And the word for the *complement* is *plērōma*. The *plērōma* is the *complement* of the city. In the New Testament itself we find in Matthew 9[16] that the word *plērōma* is used for the patch which fills in the rent in the old torn garment.

So then, if we call the Church the *plērōma* of Jesus Christ,

it means that the Church is the *complement* of Christ, that
without which Christ is not complete and cannot act.

We may think that that is a startling idea, but it is not
nearly so startling as the second great Pauline idea. In
Colossians 1[24] Paul writes: 'Now I rejoice in my sufferings
for your sake, and in my flesh I complete what is lacking in
Christ's afflictions for the sake of his body, that is, the
Church.' *I complete what is lacking in Christ's afflictions.*
That is well nigh the most startling statement in the New
Testament. How can there be anything lacking in the afflictions of Jesus Christ? How can Paul or any other human
being be in any sense said to complete them? Let us take a
human analogy. Suppose a doctor or a scientist makes some
great discovery which will lighten the world's work and ease
the world's pain, and suppose he makes it at the cost of toil
and suffering and sacrifice. Even when the discovery has
been made and the technique of it perfected, it has still to be
brought out of the laboratory into the world; it has still to be
brought to men and to the needs of men. It must therefore
be that others take that discovery, having learned it from the
man whose discovery it was, and bring it out to men all over
the world. And it often happens that those who take that
discovery out and bring its benefits to men have to suffer and
to sacrifice in order to do so. The bringing of the discovery
to men often costs just as much, and sometimes even more,
than the actual discovery of it. Now relate that to Jesus
Christ. Jesus Christ lived and died for men. 'The great
transaction's done.' But it remains unavailing until it is
brought to men. Men must be told about it; men must be
led to the Cross of Christ and the love of God. As Paul had
it when he wrote to the Romans: 'Every one who calls on the
name of the Lord will be saved. But how are men to call
upon Him in whom they have not believed? And how are
they to believe in Him of whom they have never heard? And
how are they to hear without a preacher?' (Romans 10[13, 14]).

And all down the centuries it has happened that those who brought the news and the message of Christ to others have suffered and sacrificed for their Lord. And in that suffering and sacrifice they have been filling up what is lacking in the sufferings of Christ, for by their sufferings they have been bringing the benefit of His sufferings to men. You see what that means? It means that whenever we are called upon to suffer something for Christ and for the sake of Christ, we are filling up the sufferings of our Lord—and can there be any privilege in all the world like that?

The function of the Christian—let us repeat it—is to be part of the body of Christ, to be the agent, the hands, the feet, the mouth, the mind, the heart through which Christ acts.

John Foster in *Then and Now* relates a perfect illustration of this. He heard an Indian bishop tell of the way in which an enquirer from Hinduism came to seek Christian baptism. A New Testament had come into this man's hands. He read it without any outside help or guidance. The picture of Jesus fascinated him, and moved him. He wished to take this Jesus as his master and Lord, but at first there was no idea in his mind of entering the Church. 'Then he read on . . . and felt he had entered into a new world. In the Gospels it was Jesus. His works, and His sufferings. In Acts . . . what the disciples did and thought and taught had taken the place that Christ had occupied. The Church continued where Jesus had left off at His death. "Therefore," said this man, "I must belong to *the Church that carries on the life of Christ.*" ' It is through the Church that the work of Jesus Christ continues, and, therefore, the function of the individual Christian is clear and unmistakable—he must be part of the body of Christ. It is through him that Jesus Christ evangelizes the world—or is hindered from evangelizing the world.

George Eliot has a poem about Antonio Stradivari, the

maker of the now priceless Stradivarius violins. Stradivari
did not play the violin; he only made violins, a dull enough
and a humble enough job. An artist, a painter, is belittling
the work that Stradivari did, the work, as it were, of a mere
artisan. Stradivari answers:

> *When any master holds*
> *'Twixt hand and chin a violin of mine,*
> *He will be glad that Stradivari lived,*
> *Made violins, and made them best of all.*
> . . . . .
> *While God gives them skill,*
> *I give them violins to play upon,*
> *God choosing me to help him.*
> . . . . .
> *If my hand slacked,*
> *I should rob God, since he is fullest good*
> *Leaving a blank instead of violins.*
> . . . . .
> *'Tis God gives skill,*
> *But not without men's hands. He could not make*
> *Antonio Stradivari's violins*
> *Without Antonio.*

Here is the motto of the evangelist—If my hand slacked I
should rob God. We can most literally say that the task of
evangelism is to be done for God's sake. As the hymn has it:
'For My sake and the Gospel's, go!'

So, then, we have seen that there are three things which
are clear and unmistakable—the commission of the evangelist, the sphere of the evangelist and the function of the
evangelist. Still further, *the message of the evangelist is un-
mistakably clear.* The new Testament thinkers, and especially Paul, summed up their belief in Jesus in one word—in
the word *Lord.* The creed of the early Church was contained
in one basic affirmation—*Jesus Christ is Lord.* It was the

dream and the vision that there would come a day when every
tongue would confess that Jesus Christ is Lord (Philippians 2^{11}). The test of salvation is to confess that Jesus Christ
is Lord (Romans 10^9). It is by the Holy Spirit that a man is
enabled to say that Jesus is Lord (1 Corinthians 12^3). Paul
preaches not himself, but Jesus Christ as Lord (2 Corinthians 4^5). Christians must in their heart reverence Christ as
Lord (1 Peter 3^{15}). There is one Lord, Jesus Christ
(1 Corinthians 8^6).

There is hardly any word in conventional religious
language which has been so emasculated of meaning as this
word Lord. There is a type of preacher and speaker and
writer who glibly speaks or writes of 'the Lord Jesus', or 'the
Lord Jesus Christ' in every second sentence, in a way in
which the word has become almost completely meaningless,
and in which it has become little or nothing more than a
conventional prefix to the name of Jesus. There is something
almost shocking and revolting about the glib way in which
this word Lord is so often used. Let us see what it means.
The Greek word is the word *kurios*, and *kurios* has a wide
variety of ascending meanings.

(i) It is the ordinary Greek title of respect and it is used as
Sir is used in English, Herr in German, Monsieur in French.
'I go, sir,' says the courteous but unsatisfactory son in the
parable of the two sons (Matthew 21^{30}). It is the normal
address of respect in everyday Greek language.

(ii) It is used in Greek letters in very much the same sense
in which we use the address 'My dear so and so.' The soldier
Apion begins his letter to his father Epimachus with greetings to 'his father and lord (*kurios*)', as we would say, 'My
Dear Father'.

(iii) It is regularly used of a master in contradistinction to
a slave. No man can serve two masters, two *kurioi* (Matthew 6^{24}; Luke 16^{13}). It is the title of authority.

(iv) It is regularly used in the sense of owner. It describes the man who is the absolute and undisputed owner of some person or some thing. The owner of the vineyard and the owner of the colt are *kurios* (Matthew 20[8]; 21[40]; Mark 12[9]; Luke 20[13, 15]; 19[33]). It describes absolute possession.

(v) It is used for the father of the family, the head of the household, the man who is master, *kurios*, in his own house (Epictetus, *Discourses* 3.22.3).

(vi) It has one very interesting usage. In the ancient world a woman had herself no legal rights. Therefore, when she had to enter into some contract, such as a marriage contract, or when she had to fill up some official document, such as a census return, she had to have with her her guardian, and the word for *guardian is* *kurios*. So in a marriage contract a certain Apollonia has with her her brother Apollonius as her *kurios*, her guardian.

If we were to go no further than this, it is clear to see that to call Jesus Christ *Lord* is no small thing. It is to call Him the Master whose slave I am. It is to call Him the owner whose undisputed possession I am. It is to call Him the father of that great family of which through grace I am a member. It is to call Him the great guardian of those who have no rights of their own and who stand in need of a protector against the world. But we can go further than this —much further.

(vii) *Kurios* became the standard title of the Roman Emperor, the word with which his edicts and his decrees began, the word in which his divine majesty and his imperial authority were summed up and epitomized. After examining Paul, Festus is at a loss, because he has no certain report to make to his *kurios*, his lord, that is, his Emperor, Nero (Acts 25[26]).

(viii) But we can go still further—*kurios* became the regular title which was prefixed to the names of the heathen gods. Apion, the soldier whose letter we have already quoted, writes to his father: 'I thank the lord Serapis that when I was in peril on the sea he immediately saved me.' Deissmann says of *kurios* that it was 'a divine predicate intelligible to the whole eastern world'. *Kurios* in ancient thought was the word characteristic of divinity.

(ix) Lastly, *kurios* takes the final step beyond which it could not possibly rise. In the Septuagint, the Greek translation of the Hebrew Scriptures, of the Old Testament, *kurios* is the word which is regularly used to translate the name Jehovah or Jahweh, the name of God.

And now we can see what we ought to be doing, when we call Jesus *Lord*. We are calling Him the *master* whose obedient servant we must for ever be. We are calling Him the *owner* who possesses absolutely our lives. We are calling Him the *father* whose loving and obedient sons and daughters we must be. We are calling Him the *guardian* to whom we look as the help of the helpless and the comfort of the comfortless. We are calling Him the *Emperor* whose loyal subjects we must for ever be. We are calling Him the *Divine One* whose place is in the heavenly places. We are calling Him the *God* whom we must for ever love and reverence and adore.

Surely *kurios*, Lord, is not a word to be lightly, and glibly, and conventionally, and meaninglessly taken on the lips. Surely it is a title which we must take on our lips with reverence and godly fear. And surely now we can see something of what Jesus meant when he said: 'Not everyone who says to me, Lord, Lord, shall enter the kingdom of heaven' (Matthew 7[21]).

It was with the message of Jesus Christ as Lord that the first evangelists went out to the world.

But the message of the Christian evangelist did not stop with the proclamation of Jesus Christ as *Lord*; it went on to tell of, and to offer, Jesus Christ as *Saviour*. The original creed of the ecumenical movement was: 'We confess our Lord Jesus Christ as God and Saviour.' The lordship of

Jesus Christ and the Saviourhood of Jesus Christ are insepar-
ably connected. In what is perhaps his greatest passage on
the meaning of Jesus Christ (Philippians 2^{1-11}) it is Paul's
conviction that the lordship of Jesus Christ is the direct
consequence of the fact that He emptied Himself of His
glory and that He suffered and served and died for men. It
was because Jesus Christ emptied Himself, because He took
the form of a servant, because He was born in the likeness of
men, because He humbled Himself and became obedient
unto death, even death on a cross, it was because of all that
that God highly exalted Him and gave to Him the name
Lord, the name which is above every name. Christ is Lord
because first He is Saviour. What then was this message of
Jesus Christ as Saviour? It had in it two great elements.

First, Jesus Christ is Saviour because He established once
and for all a new relationship between God and man. In
that ancient world there were many attitudes to God. There
were those who regarded religion and God as nothing else
than manifestations of debased and debasing *superstition*.
Lucretius sang the praises of Epicurus because he had
destroyed belief in the gods and had liberated men when
they were 'foully grovelling upon the ground crushed
beneath the weight of religion'. For centuries, as he saw it,
men had been 'abasing their spirits through the fear of the
gods' (Lucretius, *On the Nature of Things*, 1.61–101; vi.49).
Religion, God, on this ground was no more than a degrading
superstition out of which man must be lifted. There were
those who regarded God and religion as *convenient instru-
ments for keeping men in order*. Religion, as Polybius saw it,
was no more than 'a check upon the common people'
(Polybius vi.56). Some cunning man, the poet Critias wrote,
invented God and the fear of God to keep men under control
with the idea that the gods were secretly watching them
(Sextus Empiricus, *Against the Mathematicians* ix.54).
Varro, as Augustine tells, declared that, 'It is in the interests

of states to be deceived in religion' (Augustine, *The City of God*, iv. 27; vi5). As Gibbon had it: 'The various modes of worship which prevailed in the Roman world were all considered by the people as equally true; by the philosopher as equally false; and by the magistrate as equally useful' (*The Decline and Fall of the Roman Empire*, ch.ii). On this view God was no more than a cunningly devised fable to keep men under control. There were those who regarded God as *utterly remote*. According to the Stoics, and they were the highest thinkers of the ancient world, the first and necessary attribute of God is *apatheia*. *Apatheia* does not mean apathy; it means essential inability to feel. The Stoic argued that, if God can feel joy or sorrow, gladness or grief, pleasure or anger, it means that some one can affect God, that some one can, even for the moment, change Him. That means that some one for the moment is greater than God, for he who affects anyone is greater than the person he affects. But that cannot be, because no one can be greater than God. Therefore, it is a first necessity that God should be absolutely, and by His nature, incapable of any feeling. On this view the fact that makes God God is the fact that He cannot possibly care for men. There were many who regarded God as *the distant unknowable*. 'God,' said Antisthenes the Cynic, 'is like none else, wherefore none can know Him thoroughly from any likeness' (Lactantius, *Epitome* 14; Minucius Felix, *Octavius* xix.7). It was Plato who said that it was supremely difficult to find out anything about God, and it was impossible to tell anyone else about Him. On this view the only possible attitude is the agnosticism which is content not to know. In the Jewish world there were those who thought of God in terms of *law*. God had laid down His laws; man's relationship to God was dependent and contingent on the keeping of these laws; and God is the judge of all the earth. Such a conception can in the sensitive soul produce nothing but despair and even terror, for man can never keep the laws of God, and sin can never satisfy divine holiness. 'No man is justified before God by the law' (Galatians 3[11]). To see God as Judge and Law-giver, to think of God in terms of justice and of law, is necessarily to be for ever in terror of God, for ever in despair of satisfying His demands, for ever to follow a process of further and further estrangement in our sin from the holiness of God—which is precisely what Paul discovered in his own life. There remains still one other idea of God and of deity, and perhaps amongst the common people it was more prevalent than any other view in the ancient world. There were many who thought of God in so far as He had any contact with this earthly world at all in terms of demons, or rather, daimons. The idea was that there was a kind of blanket of these spiritual beings between men and God; these daimons formed a kind of layer in the atmosphere between men and God. God himself could not be involved in human affairs. 'He who involves God in human needs,' said Plutarch, 'does not spare His majesty, nor does he maintain the dignity and greatness of God's excellence' (Plutarch, *De Def. Orac.* 9, 414 F). Every corner in earth, every thing in nature, every power of nature had its daimon. Samuel Dill speaks of a condition of things in which there were 'gods in every grove and fountain, and on every mountain summit; gods breathing in the winds and flashing in the lightning, or the ray of sun and star, heaving in the earthquake or the November storm in the Aegean, watching over every society of men congregated for any purpose, guarding the solitary hunter or traveller in the Alps or the Sahara' (S. Dill, *Roman Society from Nero to Marcus Aurelius*, p. 482). And the point was that by far the greater number of these demonic beings were hostile to men. H. E. W. Turner says: 'It is, perhaps, hard for modern man to realize how hag-ridden was the world into which Christ came' (H. E. W. Turner, *The Patristic Doctrine of Redemption*, p. 47). Men lived in a universe where there was an unseen host of divine

powers and beings who were out to work them harm. To
this day modern missionaries tell us that one of the greatest
reliefs which Christianity brings to primitive peoples is the
discovery that there is only one all-loving God instead of an
infinite host of malignant divinities.

Into this world Jesus Christ came to tell men what God is
truly like, and thereby to establish for ever the possibility of a
quite new relationship between God and man.

It might well be said that the greatest single text in the
Bible is: 'The Word became flesh and dwelt among us'
(John 1[14]). The Greek word for *Word* is *Logos*. This word
Logos has in Greek two meanings, and there is no one
English word which has both meanings. It is for that reason
that Moffatt does not even try to translate it, but has simply:
'The Logos became flesh.'

First, *Logos* means *mind or reason*. This was a sense in
which the Greeks knew the word well. From the time of
Heraclitus of Ephesus, six hundred years before Jesus Christ,
the Greeks had been fascinated by the order of the world.
What, they asked, produces and maintains this order? What
makes the world a *cosmos* and not a *chaos*? What brings the
seasons in their unvarying appointed order? What makes
the tides ebb and flow? What keeps the stars in their courses
and solves the traffic problem of the skies? What makes this
an orderly, dependable and reliable universe in which the
same effect will always follow the same cause? What, above
all, puts reason into the being of man? The Greek answer
was that this is the result of the Logos, of the mind of God,
interpenetrating and permeating the universe. To the Greek
thinker the Logos is the mind of God. See, then, what
Christianity says. It says to the Greeks: 'For six hundred
years you have been talking about the mind, the Logos, of
God. Now the Logos has become flesh; the mind of God
has become a person. If you want to see what the mind of
God is like, look at this person Jesus Christ.' Second, *Logos*

means a *word*. What is a word? The simplest definition of a word is that *a word is the expression of a thought*. See again what Christianity is saying. It says: 'The word became flesh. If you want to see the expression of the thought of God, if you want to see what God is thinking, if you want to see the mind of God towards man, look at this person Jesus Christ.'

And when we do look at Jesus Christ, what do we see? We see one who fed the hungry and comforted the sad and opened arms of welcome to those whom the world calls sinners. That, says the Christian message, is God; that is what God is like. It cost God the life and death of His Son to tell us what He is like. As we look at the life and death of Jesus Christ, we can say: 'God loves me like that.' And immediately our whole relationship to God is changed. God is no longer the distant unknowable, the unmoved spectator, the stern judge, the pitiless law-giver, the grudging deity. God is like Jesus Christ, who died and who sacrificed His life to bring to men the knowledge of the love of God. We are reconciled to God through Jesus Christ. Our whole relationship to God is changed, and we are at home with God.

Second, Jesus Christ is Saviour because He liberates man from the power of sin. With Jesus Christ there came into the world a new dynamic. One of the most tragic features of that ancient world into which Christ came was the utter moral helplessness of which men were despairingly conscious. Men knew what they ought to be, but saw no way to change themselves. It is Persius who prays to God that he may punish tyrants that 'they may look on virtue and pine that they have lost her for ever' (*Satires* 2.31). He speaks of 'filthy Natta *numbed* with vice' (*Satires* 2.38). Men were saturated with evil—and knew it—and could do nothing about it. Seneca speaks of men 'who love and hate their vices at the same time' (*Letters* 112.3). Epictetus speaks of men's 'weakness and impotence in necessary things' (*Discourses* 2.II.1). In the *Hermotimus* (3) Lucian makes the searching and the seeking philosopher speak of the utter necessity of a hand stretched out to help (*dei cheira oregontos*). As James Denney said, the great task of Christianity, and the great achievement of Christianity, is 'to make bad men good'. One of the most wonderful sentences in the New Testament is Paul's word to the Corinthians: 'Do not be deceived; neither the immoral, nor idolaters, nor adulterers, nor homosexuals, nor thieves, nor the greedy, nor drunkards, nor revilers, nor robbers will inherit the kingdom of God. And such were some of you, but you were washed, you were sanctified, you were justified in the name of the Lord Jesus Christ and in the Spirit of our God' (1 Corinthians 6^{9-11}). Christianity came with the dynamic to lift men out of that moral helplessness which had the world in its deadly grip. It came to give men the victory over self and over sin.

Here, then, is the Christian message at its simplest and its most basic. The Christian evangelist must go out with the message of Jesus Christ as Lord and Saviour. He must tell of the Christ whose claim it is to be the Lord of life, and to whom a man must give absolute submission; he must tell of the Christ through whose sacrificial life and death men can enter into a new relationship with God, and through whose dynamic power men can achieve a life of victory in place of their frustration, their moral helplessness, and their continual defeat.

We have thought of the commission of the evangelist, of the sphere of the evangelist, of the function of the evangelist, of the message of the evangelist. And now we must think of *the task of the evangelist*. By the task of the evangelist I mean the inescapable duty of self-preparation to get this message across. This task of self-preparation falls into four parts.

The evangelist must prepare his mind. In a famous sentence Plato said, 'The unexamined life is the life not worth living'. And we may also say that the unexamined faith is the faith not worth preaching. The plain duty of the evangelist is to think things out and to think them through for himself. The gravest danger of the evangelist is that he should roll out conventional religious words and phrases which he has borrowed from others and to which he himself, if challenged, would have difficulty in attaching any meaning. The message of the evangelist must be a personal discovery. When Pilate asked Jesus: 'Are you the King of the Jews?' Jesus flashed back at him: 'Do you say this of your own accord, or did others say it to you about me?' (John 18³³, ³⁴). Is this a personal discovery or a carried, secondhand story? At Caesarea Philippi Jesus began by asking His men: 'Who do men say that I am?' They told him, and then there came the crucial question: 'But you—who do *you* say that I am?' (Mark 8²⁷⁻²⁹).

This is specially true today. We preach today to a public which is more highly educated than any public in history. They are not going to be satisfied with a glib, easy, conventional repetition of well-worn, and even outworn, phrases. Bishop Oxnam, the great American preacher, has said: 'Our generation will not be led spiritually by men it cannot respect intellectually.' Dr Ralph Sockman thinking of the great Methodist revival of religion said: 'The Wesleyan warmed heart involved the studying mind.' Wesley was adamant in his insistence. He spoke to his helpers and his preachers about reading: 'Steadily spend all morning in this employ, or at least five hours in the four and twenty.' And if a man objected that he had no taste for reading, he answered, 'Then contract a taste for it, or return to your trade!' 'The work of grace', he said, 'would die out in one generation, if the Methodists were not a reading people.' E. F. Scott has laid it down: 'The failure of Christianity as a moral force is more often than we like to think due to no other cause than intellectual sloth.'

Once John Wesley, himself a Fellow of Lincoln College, Oxford, received a note from a self-appointed, so-called evangelist telling him that 'the Lord has told me to tell you that he doesn't need your book learning, your Greek and your Hebrew'. Wesley replied: 'Thank you, sir. Your letter was superfluous, however, as I already knew the Lord has no need for my "book-learning", as you put it. However—although the Lord has not directed me to say so—on my own responsibility I would like to say to you that the Lord does not need your ignorance either.' It is of the very essence of our Christian faith that we should love the Lord with our whole mind as well as our whole heart. It is a legal maxim that genuine ignorance is a defence, but neglect of knowledge never is. The Christian must always be ready and able to give a reason for the hope that is in him (I Peter 3[15]). One of the worst debts of the Christian Church is the preacher and the evangelist who will not study the Christian faith and the book which is the word of God. It is a moral and a spiritual duty to use the minds God gave us, and the preacher who refuses to study is failing in his task.

The evangelist must prepare his material. The evangelist has to solve the problem of communication, and that cannot be solved without preparation. There are few greater insults than to arrive on a pulpit or a platform unprepared. There is a type of speaker who begins an address by saying: 'As I was coming down the road, or, as I was on my way here, I was wondering what I would speak to you about.' If he was not prepared long before that, he has no right to be on pulpit or on platform at all.

You will find a certain type of preacher and evangelist who claims that he is entirely dependent on the Holy Spirit. It is a blasphemous thing to saddle the Holy Spirit with the blame for rambling, wearisome, and unprepared effusions. Stephen Neill tells in *Men of Unity* of that great scholar A. C. Headlam, Bishop of Gloucester, at the Ecumenical Conference in Lausanne. Headlam was entirely impatient of blurred and muddled and woolly thinking, and of any attempt to substitute feeling for hard thinking. 'I deprecate', said Headlam, 'any reference to the work of the Holy Spirit.' R. C. Gillie, the great English Presbyterian preacher, once said: 'Prepare as if there was no such person as the Holy Spirit; preach as if there was nothing but the Holy Spirit.' The help of the Holy Spirit comes to him who bends every atom of mind and brain and sinew he possesses to work at the preparation of his speaking for God. Charles B. Templeton in his book *Evangelism for To-morrow* answers in one stabbing question the man who says: 'I cannot afford the time to prepare.' The one question is: 'Can you afford not to?'

I would appeal to all preachers and evangelists—write every word of your sermons, and write every word of your prayers. It is specially so in prayer. When a man rises to pray in public, it is not his own prayers but the prayers of his people that he offers to God; and, if he has not prepared them, there is every chance that after the service he will discover—as I to my shame have far more than once discovered—that he has forgotten to bring to the throne of grace the need of someone whose need is greatest of all. I do not say that we ought to read either sermons or prayers, but I say with all my heart that they ought to be written and prepared with all the devotion we possess, for it is a terrible thing to offer to God and to a congregation that which cost us nothing.

Two cooks can take precisely and exactly the same ingredients, and out of them one can produce a tempting and satisfying meal and the other can produce a stodgy or even nauseating mess. The materials the evangelist uses are always the same, but the effect of them will depend on the fidelity and the diligence with which his preparation has been done. What happens in the pulpit or on the platform depends almost entirely on what has already happened in the study and at the desk.

The evangelist must prepare himself. If a man has to prepare his mind, and if a man has to prepare his material, then quite clearly there is an utter necessity for self-discipline and self-preparation. Douglas Blatherwick in his book *A Layman Speaks* tells how the Champness Hall, Rochdale, was filled one Saturday evening for a concert given by Sir John Barbirolli and the Hallé Orchestra. As the people were leaving, a man, certainly not a churchman, said to the minister, Joseph Dowell: 'When are you going to have this place full on a Sunday night?' To which question Mr Dowell made this very meaningful reply: 'I shall have this place full on a Sunday night, when, like Sir John Barbirolli, I have with me eighty trained and disciplined men.' The man who would be an evangelist must be a trained and disciplined man. The besetting sin of the preacher and the evangelist—and well I know it of myself—is the unwillingness to sit down and work at the task of producing a form of the message of the gospel which will get across to men and women. In our ordinary day's work in trade or in commerce or in industry or in business we have to work to certain hours or we will be dismissed. In the work of the preacher and evangelist we have the responsibility that we have no master but our conscience, and no discipline but self-discipline. God give us that discipline without which no man can be a workman who has no need to be ashamed.

The evangelist must prepare his heart. No man can introduce others to Jesus Christ unless he has met Jesus Christ himself. No man can tell others of Jesus Christ unless he himself knows Jesus Christ. Only a man who is converted can convert others. To lead men into the presence of Christ a man must himself come forth from the presence of Christ. It was told of Alexander Whyte of Free St George's in Edinburgh that once after a service some one said to him: 'Dr Whyte, today you preached as if you had come straight from the presence.' And Whyte looked at the man and answered softly: 'Perhaps I did. Perhaps I did.' All the other preparations are useless without the preparation of the heart.

We have thought of the commission of the evangelist—Go! Preach! We have thought of the sphere of the evangelist—into all the world. We have thought of the function of the evangelist—to be a member of the body through which Christ acts. We have thought of the message of the evangelist—Jesus Christ, Lord and Saviour. We have thought of the task of the evangelist—the self-preparation necessary for the communication of the gospel. And, when we think of all that, the heart of even the bravest might well be daunted, if we forget the last thing of all—*the resources of the evangelist*. The evangelist has four great resources in which his weakness can become strong.

He has the *Bible* to be the inexhaustible mine from which he draws his message for others, and the inexhaustible well from which he draws comfort and strength for himself.

He has *the fellowship of the Church*. The man whose evangelism cuts him off from the Church is on the wrong way. Luther once said a strange and wise thing about Jerome, the great scholar who translated the Bible into Latin, and thus made the Vulgate which is still the Bible of the Roman Catholic Church. Jerome made his translation alone and unaided and Luther said that because he did that it was not a good translation. Jerome deliberately despoiled himself of the promise: 'Where two or three are gathered in my name, there am I in the midst of them' (Matthew 18²⁰). It is in the fellowship of kindred souls that a man can find and test his message. Dr Ralph Sockman has said: 'There has never been a significant revival of religion in the history of Christianity which has not been nurtured in a revival of Bible Study.' One of the greatest resources the evangelist can have is the fellowship of a likeminded group of people in the study of the word of God.

He has *the never closed gate of prayer*. No man's life has

ever had a foreground of effective activity, unless it has had a background of wise passivity in which he waited upon God. Bertram Pollock, Bishop of Norwich, had crowding in upon him the many duties of his office; but every day in life Bertram Pollock had his times for prayer inviolably set apart. Once his servant came to announce to him that a very distinguished visitor had come to see him. It was the Bishop's time for prayer. Very gently and very courteously he said: 'Put him in an anteroom, and ask him if he will please wait. I <u>have an appointment with God</u>.' No evangelist can fulfil his task unless he daily keeps his unbreakable appointments with God, but if he enters into God's presence by the door that no man can ever shut, then his will be the peace and power he cannot do without.

And, finally he has *the promise of the presence of his risen Lord*. We do not go to our task alone. If we had to, we could not go at all. We go with the promise and the presence, for with the command there came the promise: 'Go, therefore, and make disciples of all nations . . . and lo, I am with you always to the end of the world' (Matthew 28[19, 20])—of whom then shall we be afraid?

2

The Aim of Our Teaching

To be of value every activity must have an end product; and to be done with enthusiasm and with intelligence every activity must be done with a clear consciousness of the end product in mind. In other words a man must quite consciously know what he is trying to do; his object must be clearly defined and clearly realized. So then we must be quite clear as to the end of all our teaching.

In our work we are dealing, not with things, but with persons; and therefore it is quite clear that our aim must always be to produce a certain kind of person. W. H. Davies, the tramp poet, tells of a conversation with a small boy. He said to the boy: 'What are you going to be when you grow up?', expecting the answer, an engine-driver, or a policeman, or a doctor or a lawyer or some such thing. 'What am I going to be when I grow up?' said the lad in a tone of voice of one faced with a silly question. 'Why, of course, a man!' And of course the end of life is manhood. Agesilaus the Spartan king was asked: 'What shall we teach our boys?' His prompt answer was: 'That which will be most useful to them when they are men.' So, then, our aim can be put in one sentence —*our aim is to produce men* in the true sense of the term. But we must further define this aim in the context of the Christian faith and of the situation in which our work lies.

(1) We must produce *a young man who knows what he believes and who is able to state and to defend that belief.* To do that there must be certain things in our programme.

(*a*) There must be *systematic instruction* in Scripture and in the Creed. It must be clearly laid down that the kind of meeting to which different speakers are invited each week to give an unrelated talk are of very little value educationally. Far be it from me to be either critical or cruel, but it often seems to me that a YMCA can pride itself on the wrong things. It can, for instance, pride itself on a big midweek service. That is an excellent thing in itself; but when one looks round on such a service one could sometimes count on the fingers of two hands the number of young men under thirty who are present; and in the nature of things at that kind of meeting systematic instruction is impossible. The last thing anyone would want to do is to stop such a service; but, if we are to fulfil our educational task of communicating the Gospel, there must be systematic instruction in the Christian faith.

(*b*) There must be *expert instruction* in the Christian belief and doctrine. In the teaching of any subject we bring in the man who has studied it and who knows it. The expert exists so that we may make use of him; and what is true of all other subjects is also true of Christian instruction.

(*c*) There must be teaching which is *a dialogue and not a monologue*. That is to say, teaching must be not so much telling a young man what to believe as helping him to discover it for himself. There must be ample room for two-way question-and-answer and for discussion, because, if there is not, two things will happen. First, we may well be asking and answering questions which the young person is not asking at all; and, second, no opportunity is being given for the young person to express his own faith and belief.

(*d*) It must always be remembered that what we are seeking to inculcate is *a particular kind of knowledge*. There are two kinds of belief. The one is the assent of the mind and is intellectual belief; the other is the assent of the total personality, and, for want of a better name, we may call it practical

belief. To take an example—I believe that the square of the
hypotenuse of a right-angled triangle equals the sum of the
squares on the other two sides, but it makes no difference to
me, but I believe that six and six make twelve and therefore I
will resolutely refuse to pay one shilling and two pence for
two sixpenny bars of chocolate. The one kind of belief I
accepted with my mind; on the other kind of belief I found
and base my whole life and living. The kind of knowledge
which we teach is not the knowledge in which a man rests
only his mind; it is the kind of knowledge to which he com-
mits his whole life. A discussion group should not be simply
a good-going argument; it should be a group of people
intent on finding out how to live.

(2) We must produce *a young man who is a man of principle.*
To put it in another way, we must produce a young man who
is never ashamed to show whose he is and whom he serves.
This is not to say that we want to produce a priggish person
who in season and out of season, as it were, flaunts his
Christianity in people's faces. But it is to say that we want to
produce a young man who never leaves anyone in any doubt
as to where he stands.

A few years ago I had a student who was a brilliant
engineer. He had had a considerable part in the development
of the jet engine. Any kind of career was open to him, and
any kind of financial gain was also open to him. He had
already held a high position in the engineering faculty of the
University. He decided to give all this up to enter the
Ministry of the Church of Scotland. It was necessary for me
to see him to settle certain matters about his course and
curriculum. To save him the trouble of travelling out to the
suburb of Glasgow where I live, I arranged to meet him in a
city hotel to have a meal with him there. We met; he went
into the dining-room; the order was taken; the waiter
brought the first course; and before he ate Jack bowed his
head and said his grace before meat. How many of us say

grace before meat in a restaurant or an hotel? It is not so much the matter of saying grace before meat in a restaurant; that in itself is a comparatively small and unimportant thing. It is all that it symbolically stands for; it is the willingness to show even there where the heart lies and to whom the loyalty is given.

There is no doubt that the tendency is in so many cases to play down our Christian faith and witness. We tend to say or to imply: 'Yes, I'm a Christian, but really it doesn't matter very much. Don't mind me.'

And the tragedy is that so many people are only waiting for a lead. I well remember an incident from my school days. We had been sitting an examination; when the examination was over, although we well knew that we should not have done so, instead of returning to the class rooms we went for a walk. We were in due course carpeted. Down the line the headmaster went asking why we had done this. And he received as ingenious a series of excuses as you could hear from the first half dozen or so. Then he came to a lad who, as it happens, is now a Professor of Economics in a Welsh university. 'Why did you do this?' said the headmaster. 'I have no excuse,' Duncan said. And one by one after him everyone admitted his error. The example of that lad had turned a series of shuffling cowards into a series of lads brave enough to admit their fault. It was a small enough thing, but it was a demonstration of the fact that time and time again what is wanted is simply someone to take the lead.

It is our task to produce young men of principle who in any company are not ashamed to show whose they are and whom they serve.

(3) We must produce *young men who are built into the Church.* I do not think that it is too much to say that the YMCA must always be looking beyond itself. The YMCA cannot be a substitute for the Church; it must be a road and a channel into the Church. When we think of it this way it is

worth while to think just what the Church is, for in this we
are not thinking of any denomination but of the Church.
There are four New Testament words which tell us much
about the Church.

There is the word *ekklēsia*, from which of course our word
ecclesiastic comes. This word *ekklēsia* has five lines of
meaning.   *ΕΚΚΛΗΟΊΑ*

(i) In the Old Testament the word *ekklēsia* is the word
which is regularly used for *the congregation of the people.*
When the Old Testament speaks about the congregation of
Israel, it is almost always thinking of the people assembled to
listen to the voice of God spoken through God's servant
Moses. There is our first line; the Church is a company of
people met to listen to the voice of God. It is a company of
people saying: Lord what wilt thou have me, to do?

But the word *ekklēsia* has a Greek meaning. In Athens the
ekklēsia was the governing body of the people. Theoretically
it consisted of every Athenian citizen who had not lost his
rights as a citizen. It was summoned to its meetings by a
trumpeter who went through the streets inviting the citizens
to attend, and in fact the *ekklēsia* consisted of those who had
accepted the invitation to come. The Church then consists
of those who have accepted the invitation of God.

But still further. The word *ekklēsia* can mean a company
of those who have been picked out. The Church then consists of that company of people whom the grace of God has
called and who have answered to that call.

(ii) In the New Testament the Church is often called the
koinōnia, and *koinōnia* means *fellowship*. So then the Church
is a fellowship. In the Church there ought to be a together-
ness which exists nowhere else. The Church ought to be
one united band of brothers.

So often it is anything but that; and the tragedy is that
when Church people are at variance it is so often about
things which do not matter. In the ancient world the heathen

said with wondering amazement: See how these Christians love one another! Could they say so now?

Once a man came to Dr Johnson. He worked in a factory where they made paper and pack-thread. He had taken a sheet of paper and a little length of pack-thread to tie up a parcel, and he had convinced himself that he had committed a deadly sin. He went on and on about this to Dr Johnson until at last the Doctor burst out upon him: 'Man, stop bothering about paper and pack-thread when we are all living together in a world that is bursting with sin and sorrow.' How often Church people are bothering about paper and pack-thread when we are all living together in a world that is bursting with sin and sorrow.

The Church's disunities are a denial of Christian fellowship. In particular this is so in regard to the Table of our Lord. There is a tragic thing in W. E. Sangster's biography, a thing which might have had the most serious consequences for the Church of Christ. In the 1914–18 war Sangster was in the Army. Even then he was a convinced Christian and even then in the most difficult and discouraging circumstances he made his witness unflinchingly to Christ. On Sunday evenings the Church of England padre held a little Bible Class in the camp. About half a dozen attended, not without the amused laughter and jeers of the others. The time for the celebration of the Sacrament came, and the Sacrament was refused to Sangster and to his friend Fred Kerry because the one was a Methodist and the other a Baptist. There is no point in denying that the scandal of disunity does infinite damage to the Church. It would have been understandable if the young Sangster had turned his back on religion there and then. The sooner the Churches all learn that the Table of the Sacrament is not their Table but the Table of the Lord Jesus Christ the better. Fellowship is a mockery when Christians cannot share in the Church's central act of worship.

(iii) The Church is *the Body of Christ*. There has been too much mystery-mongering about this great phrase. It means that the Church is the body through which Jesus Christ has to act. Jesus Christ is not now here in the flesh; therefore if He wants something done He has to get a man or a woman to do it for Him. Jesus Christ wants a young man taught; nothing will teach that young man unless one of us is prepared to do so. Through the Church Christ acts, and without the Church He cannot act. The Church has to be hands and feet to do Christ's work on earth.

(iv) The Church is the company of people each of whom can say *Jesus Christ is Lord*. The essence of membership of the Church is the acceptance of Jesus Christ as Lord.

So then we have to build the young man into the Church, the Church which is the listening people of God, the Church which has accepted the invitation of God, the Church which is a fellowship in Christ, the Church which is the instrument of Christ, the Church which is pledged to obedience to Jesus Christ.

(4) We must produce *a young man who is deeply, consciously and deliberately involved in the world*. Here we are up against a difficulty. The idea that the highest kind of Christianity involves total withdrawal from the world dies hard. The hermit in the desert, the monk in his cell, the nun in the convent—this is the common idea of what we might call plus-Christianity. This idea began in the third century. It was then that the holy men so-called began to see the Christian life as a withdrawal from the world. We get two typical manifestations of this. There were those extraordinary creatures called the pillar saints. They lived on the top of pillars which year by year they increased a little in height, totally separated from the world. There were the *inclusi*, the enclosed ones. They lived in cells of which the opening had been blocked up with bricks so that they could not get out, and there was left only a tiny slit through which the bare

minimum of food could be passed to them. They lived in deliberate starvation and emaciation; they lived in deliberate filth. Jerome writes to Paula: Shall Paula deliberately tempt Satan by taking a bath? It was quoted as an example of supreme holiness of one of them that the lice dropped from him as he walked. If they did not go as far as that, they did withdraw into the monasteries and the convents and the nunneries, where they remained in prayer and praise withdrawn from the world. This was the highest manifestation of Christianity. They were, as someone has said, so heavenly minded that they were no earthly use.

To begin with, one can only say that no life ever lived on earth is more unlike the life of Jesus. Jesus was a tradesman; He lived the ordinary life of man and shared the ordinary toils and joys of a man; He was happy at a wedding-feast and thoroughly at home in a fisherman's cottage; He was such a happy person that they called Him a glutton and a drunkard. Jesus was involved in life up to the hilt. The plain fact is that withdrawal from the world would have made the doing of His divine work completely impossible.

The true Christian attitude to involvement in the world is found in the commonest word in the New Testament to describe the Christian. Again and again the Christians are called *saints*. It is a misleading translation because it tends to make us think of a figure in a stained-glass window and of that kind of withdrawn Christianity about which we have been thinking. The Greek word is *hagios*, which is regularly translated *holy* in other places, and which in Hebrew is *kadosh*. The basic meaning of this word is *different*; it describes that which is different, other, separate from ordinary persons or things. Remember the Sabbath day to keep it *different* from other days. The Temple is holy because it is different from other buildings; a priest is holy because he is different from other men; a sacrificial animal is holy because it is different from other animals; God's book is holy because it is different from other books; and supremely God is holy because He belongs to a different sphere of being and is different from humanity.

Basically, then, to say that the Christian is a *saint* is to say that he is different from other people. But this difference is to be expressed not in withdrawal but in involvement. The New Testament does not speak of the saints in a monastery or the saints in a convent; it speaks of the saints in Rome, in Philippi, in Ephesus; the difference is expressed not in withdrawal from the world but in involvement in the world.

The Christian is a man who insists on bringing his Christianity to bear upon that situation within the world in which he finds himself. This has certain necessary consequences.

(*a*) The Christian must be involved in the *community*. It is the plain duty of the Christian to be deeply involved in such things as local government, in politics, and in Trade Unions' affairs. It is here that we have indeed one of the disasters of the present situation. We complain about the quality of men who discharge the duties of local government; we complain about the lack of principle and conviction in politics; we complain about the selfishness and irresponsibility of at least some Trade Union practice. But the plain fact is that in a democracy a people gets the leaders and rulers it chooses; and Christians have often refused to become involved. A Trade Union can become Communist-dominated for the simple reason that only Communists will attend meetings and accept office with enthusiasm.

I am not pleading that the Church should preach politics; still less am I saying that the Christian should identify himself with any one political party. What I am saying is that the Christian should willingly and conscientiously accept all the duties of a Christian and express his Christianity within them.

In this we have never realized the potential of the Church. In Scotland there are almost 5,000,000 people; of these five million about 1,500,000 adults are full members of the Church of Scotland. It is quite clear that if these people united in action and in witness they could Christianize public life within a generation.

The Christian is failing in his duty as a Christian if he does not bring his Christianity to bear upon the whole community situation in which he lives. Of course, it will mean the sacrifice of time and leisure and pleasure, but it is an inescapable obligation. The Christian ought to be the leaven in the community by which the character of the whole community is changed.

(b) This will also bring us *a Christian approach to work*, which is one of the prime necessities of the present situation.

The Old Testament and the New Testament differ in their view of work. In the old story of the Creation, work becomes an unpleasant necessity. In the Garden, according to that old story, work is a condemnation. 'In the sweat of thy brow shalt thou eat thy bread.' In the New Testament, work becomes an expression of a man's Christianity.

Here Christianity entered into two backgrounds. Graeco-Roman civilization was founded on slavery. It was beneath the dignity of a Roman citizen to work; that was the function of slaves. Hebrew thought moved in entirely the opposite direction. 'He who does not teach his son a trade,' the Jewish teachers said, 'teaches him to steal.' According to Jewish principles no man might take any money for preaching or teaching; he had to make his living at a trade. So you find Rabbis who were tailors, bakers, shoemakers, perfumers, all kinds of things. Paul was a tent-maker, and it was his pride that he took money from no man, and that he satisfied his own needs with the work of his own hands.

Of course, the supreme example of this is Jesus Himself. For thirty out of His thirty-three years He lived in Nazareth and He was the village carpenter there. It was as the carpenter that they knew Him. When they heard the wonder of

His words, their reaction was: is not this the carpenter?
And there is a legend that Jesus of Nazareth made the best
ox-yokes in all Palestine, and that men came from all over to
buy them. There seems to me to be little doubt that the
story of the parable of the talents as Jesus told it has autobiography in it. In it the master says to the good servants:
'Well done, good and faithful servant! You have discharged
a small duty faithfully: I will trust you with a much bigger
one.' If Jesus had not faithfully discharged the duties of the
carpenter's shop in Nazareth He would never have been
given the supreme duty of being the Saviour of the world. If
you like to put it so, Jesus was a working man.

Jesus's whole attitude to work is summed up in one of the
unwritten sayings, one of these sayings which never got into
any Gospel but which have been later discovered. This
saying runs: 'Cleave the wood and you will find me, raise the
stone and I am there.' This means that when the carpenter is
working with the wood and the mason with the stone, Jesus is
there; in the common routine tasks of life the presence of the
Risen Lord is with us.

Here then we are given the Christian philosophy of work,
which is quite simply that every task must be done in such a
way that it is fit to present to Jesus Christ. In other words all
work is done for Him. It may be that the Church itself has
been to blame for the failure of people at large to have a
really Christian view of work. The title 'a servant of God'
has been far too narrowly interpreted. It has been assumed
that a servant of God is a preacher or a teacher or a surgeon
or someone who is engaged in work which is obviously great
and important. But look at it this way. God obviously wants
His people to be healthy and happy; therefore clearly the
doctor and the surgeon are doing the work of God. But
clearly people cannot be healthy and happy unless they are
well fed, well clothed and well shod. Therefore, the farmer,
the tailor, the shoemaker are doing the work of God. But the

products of the farmer and the craftsman must reach the public; therefore all the people who are involved in the intricate business of transporting them and selling them are doing the work of God. All useful work is work for God. That a service is apparently small and apparently unseen is no indication at all that it is unimportant. The failure of the smallest nut or screw or bolt or wire in some quite unseen part of the engine can render a motor-car quite useless. Ordinary people doing ordinary jobs must be helped to see that they too are servants of God.

It is clear to see what a difference this would make. We are living in an age of shoddy workmanship; we are living in an age when it is the deliberate policy to do as little as possible and to get as much as possible. We are living in an age when it is almost true to say that to do an honest day's work is the best way to get oneself dismissed or to be the cause of a strike. If we could do something towards producing a generation of young men with a Christian conception of work we would be doing something which would change the face of society.

If this is to be done it means deep involvement in all the affairs of the community. As Charles Péguy the French thinker has said: 'Everything must begin in mysticism and end in politics.' We have only to remember how deeply the Hebrew prophets were committed to the gospel of social justice. The book of Amos repeatedly reads like a political manifesto. We have the dream; we have to create the society in which the dream can become true, and we can only do that by being deeply involved in it.

Before we leave this matter of involvement we have one question left to ask. *Wherein lies this difference which the Christian life must display?* Essentially the difference lies in the phrase of Paul—*in Christ*. The Christian life is lived in Christ. To put that at its simplest it means that the Christian is for ever aware of the presence of Jesus Christ, that the only concern of the Christian is how what he does will seem to Christ and how what he says will seem to Christ, that his sole standard of judgement and value of anything is Christ, that his continual question is, Lord, what do you want me to?, that he has become a man who never again wants to do as he likes but who wants always to do as Jesus Christ likes. The Christian is a man to whom the presence of Christ is the most real thing in the world.

(c) We may put this same truth in another way. We must try to produce *a young man who has a correct set of values in this world*. There is apparently a certain insanity in the world's values. A popular singer may get a salary five times as large as the Prime Minister. A comedian turns down an offer of £1,500 a week for an engagement as being not worth his while, while a nurse cannot get a rise in her pay of one shilling in the pound. Now although entertaining may well contribute to the health and happiness of mankind this rule of remuneration does suggest that we have got our priorities wrong.

To put it at its very simplest, we want to produce a young man who will judge life's decisions by other than financial standards. How do people choose their job, or their trade, or their profession nowadays? Almost wholly on the question, What do I get out of it? Almost never on the answer to the question, What does God want me to do with my life? Almost always on the standard, What use can I make of others?, almost never on the standard, How can I be used for others? We would be doing something of infinite value if we could do something to produce a generation which put its values on service and on the acceptance of the will of God. There is many a man who makes himself a glittering career and who in so doing misses his destiny.

(d) Lastly, we must seek to produce *a young man who is always aware that there is a life to come*. If there is no life to come, then we might as well eat, drink and be merry, for tomorrow we die. It is only in the light of eternity that we get our values right in time.

I would like to tell you a story of a certain young man who was a student of mine until only last year. He is not a boy; he had a distinguished career in the army before he came to us, although he is still a very young man. He finished his divinity course, and he was due to be ordained as a preacher of the Gospel. In Scotland at such a time a young man appears before the Presbytery in a Church before what is usually a very large congregation. He takes the vows and he is ordained by the laying-on of hands; and a charge is given to him by a senior minister. I had grown to know this lad intimately for a variety of reasons and he asked me if I would give the charges. Three days before the service his father dropped dead. His father's funeral was fixed for the day of his ordination. No presbytery would have insisted on proceeding on such an occasion as that; any presbytery would gladly have postponed the trial and the ordeal of the day of ordination. Douglas chose to go on. I spoke to him and I asked him if he was sure that he wanted to proceed in such tragic circumstances. He is a happy soul, always with a smile. He looked at me with that smile of his, rather as if I were the one needing the comfort and not he. He said to me: 'Of course I'm going on. Dad lived for this day; his one desire was to see me an ordained minister.' And then he went on: 'And the one thing I'm sure of is that Dad will have a front seat in the grandstand tonight.' I do not think that I will ever forget that; and that is what Christian conviction can do for a boy.

Our efforts will not be in vain if we can produce young men conscious deeply of the unseen cloud of witnesses who compass them about, and to whom the unseen world is as real as this world of space and time.

Let me tell you another thing. I have another student. He is a slightly older man and he gave up a very good position in the shipping world to come to us. Academically he is having a sore struggle. He has a beautiful wife and three lovely children. About three months ago another child arrived. It was a mongol, a semi-idiot child. Stewart and his wife loved that child as few children have been loved. He told no one of his trouble except his closest friends. 'We don't want anyone's sympathy,' he said. Thirteen weeks the child lived surrounded with love and then died— mercifully, as anyone would agree. I went to see him and Sheila in their home. They talked quite naturally of little John without a trace of bitterness and with nothing of tears. Then Sheila said: 'We have been searching the Bible for a text, and we have found one—in Hebrews: "Some there be that have entertained angels unawares".' That is what Christianity can do for a young couple in distress.

It is thus utter happiness of faith that we must try to produce.

One last word—I have talked much about our work, our message, our duty, our challenge, but I have talked very little about ourselves. There is one thing left to say. In his biography of his father, Paul Sangster has a chapter on W. E. Sangster as a preacher; and he heads it with a quotation from the American Methodist Bishop, Bishop Quayle. Quayle wrote:

Preaching is the art of making a sermon and delivering it. Why no, that is not preaching. Preaching is the art of making a preacher, and delivering that. Preaching is the outrush of soul in speech. Therefore the elemental business in preaching is not with the preaching but with the preacher. It is no trouble to preach, but a vast trouble to construct a preacher. What, then, in the light of this is the task of a preacher? Mainly this, the amassing of a great soul so as to have something worth while to give—the sermon is the preacher up to date.

Here is the last word. We come back to the eternal truth— we cannot preach what we do not know; we cannot introduce anyone else to one whom we have never met or who is a stranger to us.

We shall do nothing unless we know Jesus Christ and commit ourselves to Him. And by ourselves we can do nothing, but with Him all things are possible.

3

The People We Teach

THE final commandment of the Risen Christ to his disciples was:

Go therefore and make disciples of all nations, baptizing them in the name of the Father and of the Son and of the Holy Spirit, teaching them to observe all that I have commanded you and lo, I am with you always to the close of the age (Matthew 28[19, 20]).

If this is so, then the Christian Church can never escape the double imperative of its Lord: *Go! Teach!* The teaching duty of the Church is a primary obligation of the Church.

One of the main tragedies of the modern Church has been its extraordinary failure to accept and to fulfil this teaching mission. We live in the age of the topical sermon, in which the preacher just as often begins from the newspaper as from the Bible.

The Church can never escape its teaching duty; least of all can it escape it today.

In face of this what are we to teach? That is a question to the answer of which we shall have to address ourselves later in our study; but thus early there is a principle which we must lay down.

There are two kinds of teaching.

(a) There is the teaching which teaches a man to make a *vocational* living. That kind of teaching is entirely necessary. You will remember Robert Burns' advice to a young friend:

Then gather gear by every wile
That's justified by honour;
To catch Dame Fortune's golden smile
Attendant wait upon her,
Not for to hide it in a hedge,
Or for the train attendant,
But for the glorious privilege
Of being independent.

It is a first duty in life to reach a position in which a man can support himself and those dependent on him. Teaching to make a living is a first essential—but it is not the main part of our work, however much we are bound to assist it in every way we can.

(*b*) There is the kind of teaching which teaches a man to live. The best definition of education is that education is the transmission of life to the living by the living. This kind of teaching teaches a man a whole attitude to life. It is necessary to do much more than teach a man the skills and crafts and techniques and knowledge by the exercise of which he can make a living. He must be taught above all the spirit in which he is to use them. Will he use them diligently or carelessly? Will he be a conscientious or a shoddy workman? Will he use them responsibly or irresponsibly? Will he use them selfishly or in the spirit of a service? Will he be a ruthless individualist, shouldering others out of his way, and intent only on the fulfilment of his own ambition, or will he be dedicated to the service of his fellow men? Will he live on the principle, 'I'm all right, Jack', or will he be unable to rest when he has too much and others have too little? His attitude to life will decide that, and it is life that we are bound to teach.

Grenfell of Labrador needed help for the medical work he was doing in that country. He came with a request for help to one of the head nurses in the famous John Hopkins Hospital in America. He said to her: 'If you want to have the time of your life, come with me and run a hospital next summer for the orphans of the Northland. There will not be a cent of money in it for you, and you will have to pay your own expenses. But I will guarantee that you will feel a love for life you have never before experienced. It's having the time of one's life to be in the service of Christ.' She went, and when she came back she wrote: 'I never knew before that life was good for anything but what one could get out of it. Now I know that the real fun lies in seeing how much one can put into life for others.'

In that story you have typified the two kinds of education. That nurse was educated to make a living in the schools and the colleges and the hospitals in which she worked and studied, and she was well educated for she had reached a responsible position. But she was educated in living by Wilfred Grenfell—which is a very different thing. And it is education in living which is our great task.

The obligation to teach is clear; the ultimate aim of teaching is equally clear. The obligation comes inescapably from the imperative of Jesus; the aim is to enable the people we teach really to live.

Let us then go on to look at the people amongst whom our work lies; and here, of course, it is on boys and young men that we must fix our attention, for it is they who are our chief concern. We shall find that they fall into five classes. We shall see that the first four classes present us with an obligation and a challenge and a duty and a responsibility, but not with any insuperable problem. Obviously the supreme problem of teaching is the problem of communication; and the members of the first four groups speak the same language as we do. They may not agree with what we say; they may not wish to listen to what we say; they may have no use for what we say; they may be actively hostile to what we say; they may rejoice in what we say; but they do know what we are talking about; they do recognize the terms we use; they

do have a background of thought which is not so very different from our own. With them the problem of persuasion
may be very difficult, but the problem of communication
hardly arises. But in the case of the fifth group, when we
come to them, we shall see that they do not speak the same
language; all our thoughts and the expression of these
thoughts are quite foreign to them; they will simply have no
idea what we are talking about. That which we hold precious
is to them completely irrelevant; it is something to which
they are not hostile, but which appears to them totally
irrelevant.

In presenting the Home Mission report to the Methodist
Conference in 1957 the late W. E. Sangster said:

We are appalled by the granite indifference of the artisan masses
to our faith. . . . Our own Church membership has decreased
again. While there are places where the work is gloriously reviv-
ing, there is no obvious revival of religion in the nation as a whole.

It is not militant opposition. Anyone who has consistently
visited in a new building-area, or tackled some of these great new
blocks of flats in the inner belt of our large city, knows quite
plainly what I mean. 'You like going to Church on Sunday
night? All right, I'm not stopping you. I like to go to the pictures
or stay in and see the "telly".'

The simple truth is that these people feel no need for the goods
which they think we are offering. We offer in Christ's name
forgiveness, and at present they feel no need of it. We talk about
peace and joy, and they say: 'I get along all right.'

Alas, we seem to live in different worlds, to talk different
languages and to move in different circles . . . and the circles do
not intersect.

(1) The first group consists of those *who are Christian and
who are within the faith*. What can we do for them, and what
must we do for them? We can keep them that way and we
can enable them to travel a little farther along the way upon
which they have already begun. It is here that we may stop

for a moment to think out the real use of the Church and the
real use of an institution like the YMCA for all such. For
such the Church can do five things.

(*a*) The Church can bring to bear an influence upon them
which, if it is brought early enough, they can never wholly
escape. If they begin life in a Christian fellowship, they are
marked for ever by that beginning. You will remember the
famous claim of Ignatius Loyola: 'Give me a child for the
first seven years of his life, and I do not care who gets him
afterwards.' The great value of integration into a Christian
fellowship is that when the young man goes out to the
temptations and the seductions of the world he has an unseen
and an almost unconscious prophylactic which protects
him from the infection of the world. Our task is to bring to
bear upon young people that influence which never wholly
leaves them. It is the experience of life that when a lad is
brought up in a good home and in a good Christian fellowship, when he goes out into the world and is tempted as he is
bound to be, into his mind unbidden there comes a text, a
verse of a hymn, a face, a memory, and saves him in the
moment of danger. That is one reason why there is every
cause to think of your work beginning with lads of twelve so
that the seed may be sown and the leaven given a chance to
work as early as possible.

(*b*) The Church is the custodian of the truth. In the
Protestant Church the individual is allowed and indeed
encouraged to think for himself; but that does not mean that
he can reach any conclusions to which a misguided mind
may lead him. His thinking is done within the context of
the Church; and he has in the Church's teaching both a
basis from which he may start and a touchstone by which he
may test all things. There is a very real sense in which we
hold the Church's faith whatever our personal beliefs may be.
For a long time I was very unwilling to recite the Creed, and
for a long time I would not use it at any Church service in

D

once again we Americans are individualists whereas in N.T. we're incorporated into the body

which I was taking part, because there are certain things in it which I could not honestly say that I believed. Then in a book by F. R. Barry, the Bishop of Southwell, I came on something which to me was an illumination. The declaration with which the Creed was originally introduced was not *I believe*, but, *We believe*. Here is something that I can say. There may be things which I myself cannot accept and believe but they are part of the structure and heritage of the faith of the Church, and I can declare the Church's faith. The Church gives the young man a basis and foundation and test for thought.

(*c*) The Church provides friendship, and it provides friendship anywhere throughout not only the country but the world. There is nothing in this world so valuable as to have a group of like-minded people into which we can go and with whom we can talk; and when the Church is as it ought to be it is just that. And—greater yet—the Church is such that wherever the young person goes he will find such a group waiting for him into which he can enter without any introduction and find friends. The Church is the provider of fellowship and of a fellowship which exists all over the world.

(*d*) The Church provides a sphere of service. There is nothing like a job to do to cement a person into any institution. Somehow he must express his faith in action; and the more he expresses it the stronger it will become. The Church provides these avenues of service which are of the greatest value in strengthening a man's faith by helping him to express it.

So then we in the YMCA can give to the young person who is already within the faith an influence which will keep him on the road on which he has begun, a basis and a touchstone for his faith, a fellowship in which all over the country and the world he can express the faith he holds, and a sphere in which he can both express and strengthen his faith by the service of his fellow men.

(2) The second group is composed of those who are *openly and actively hostile to the Christian faith and even violently opposed to it*. In this group there is for instance the atheist who will not accept the fact of God at all. Once again, communication with this group is not difficult. It will often happen that the man who claims to be an atheist will know the Bible better than we who profess to be Christians. What we can do for them is that we can provide a place and a forum where things can be thrashed out, where conversation and discussion can take place. In point of fact the YMCA can do that much better than the Church. There is always the suspicion that the Church's main interest is in making members, and the man with such beliefs might well not wish to enter it at all, but the YMCA can provide a meeting-place for free discussion—always with this proviso that we must first equip our own members in their own faith before they can face any such encounter and lest they be unable to give a reason for the hope that is in them.

(3) There are the young men *who once had some Church connection, and who in their earlier days were brought up in the orbit of the Church and who have drifted away*. These exist in very large numbers, for the biggest leakage in the Christian Church of all branches is at twelve. Here again there is no real problem of communication; once again we are dealing with a group which speaks our language and which knows our tradition.

There are two things which we can do here. (*a*) We can begin our work with lads as young as twelve, and we can make every attempt to get hold of them when they will not enter the organized Church. (*b*) It may well be that such young people will continue to frequent the YMCA in many of its activities while they have nothing to do with the Church. It may well be that the YMCA will have to do more to see that the spiritual claims of the Association are put fairly and squarely before those who use its other facilities, for it is there, if anywhere, that this type is likely to be found.

(4) There are a certain number of young people *who accept the Christian religion but who see no necessity for the Church.* Some time ago the *Sunday Post* published a whole column of verdicts on religion by young people and teenagers. A student aged twenty says:

The ideals the Church preaches are all right, but you don't need a Church to know how to behave.

An art student aged twenty writes:

I believe I can stay in contact with God without doing it publicly.

A girl student aged twenty writes:

I think most ministers don't have a very realistic approach to religion. I'm not an atheist, but I think you can be a Christian without going to Church.

It may be that this attitude is more widespread than we think. In theory it is easy enough to show its error. Take an analogy. Suppose the country was at war, and suppose there was a lad who conceived it his duty to fight for his country. Suppose him to say: 'I wish to fight for my country; but I absolutely refuse to join the army; I'll do my fighting on my own.' It is quite clear that anything he could do would be ineffective and useless. If we are on any particular side the natural and inevitable thing to do is to ally ourselves in fellowship and in work with those who stand for the same thing. Unity is strength. If we believe in Christianity, then the obvious step is to take our stand with those who have the same belief, that is, with the Church.

It may well be that the YMCA can do much for these people, for they may well come to it, when they will not come to the Church. And it may well be that we shall get more out of these people by asking for their help for our work rather than by offering them something which we want to give them. There is a great story in Numbers about a man called Hobab. When Moses set out on the desert journey he wanted Hobab's help and he wanted Hobab to come with Israel. So he tried to persuade him to join them. 'Come with us,' he said, 'and we will do you good.' And Hobab refused. Then Moses tried again. 'Come with us,' he said, 'for we need you to be eyes for us on the desert journey', and Hobab came. The appeal for help did what the offer of benefit could not do.

It may be that our best approach to this kind of person is rather to appeal for their help than to offer our help. And it may be that working together will in the end beget worshipping together.

(5) The last of the groups is the group which forms the challenge, the challenge which so far the Church and the YMCA has signally failed to accept. There is a very large number of young people nowadays *to whom religion is nothing and for whom the Church does not exist*. There is a lost generation to whom Christianity means nothing at all. They are not hostile to the Church; for them the Church is simply irrelevant. Of course there have been interesting experiments; of course there are places in which this lost generation is being contacted, but neither the Church nor the YMCA has ever made any deliberate effort to go out and get them; there has been no planning and no policy of seeking to win them. They are the teddy boys; the café haunters; the leather-jacketed motor-bicycle speedsters; the beatniks; the experimenters with reefers and other drugs; those who can work themselves up to hysteria at the appeal of a popular singer; those who are on the fringe of crime and amongst whom delinquency and destructiveness is rife. It is questionable if they have ever thought of the Church in their lives.

In the same column of verdicts the *Sunday Post* quoted some sayings of such young people. A lad of sixteen says:

Church drives me up the wall. It's not worth getting out of bed for. None of my pals go to church either.

A nineteen-year-old clerk says:

I don't believe in God. I don't believe in religion whatsoever.

An apprentice joiner says:

I never go to Church. It's just a waste of time.

A nineteen-year-old apprentice C.A. says:

Christianity is a thing of the past. It's dying out rapidly. I won't be sorry to see it go. Church? Not for me.

A nineteen-year-old science student says:

Religion has no place in modern society. They repeat the same things over and over again.

These people have at least thought about the matter enough to give a verdict; but there are others who, asked about the Church, would simply look with blank incredulity, quite unable to understand what the questioner was talking about. Let us look at the characteristics of this lost generation.

(i) It is an age which is *adrift*. It does not really believe in anything. There are no great principles for which it would be prepared to die, and there are no causes for which it is prepared to live. In the ultimate sense it is quite aimless and quite purposeless.

(ii) Basically, it is an age which is *afraid*. Some short time ago I made a discovery. I got myself involved in the campaign for nuclear disarmament. When I first became involved in it, I thought that those who went on marches and who embarked on passive civil disobedience were idealists willing to take risks and to make sacrifices for a great cause, the cause of world peace. I have not the slightest doubt that that is true of some, but I made the discovery that very many of those young people who are involved in that movement are involved for no other reason than that they are afraid. It is survival they are interested in far more than world peace. Their dominating motive is none other than fear.

(iii) Basically, it is an age which *has never known security*. A young person said to Margaret Avery: 'The basic difference between your generation and ours is that ours has never known what it is to feel safe.' Thirty or forty years ago there was certainly insecurity in the economic sense of the term, as anyone who have lived through the middle 1930's well remembers. That was bad and even tragic; but there never was the ultimate insecurity which feels, not that it is going to be unemployed, but that the world in which it is living is liable literally to disintegrate at any moment. Our generation well knew insecurity of employment and the like; this generation since it can think at all has known the insecurity of possible annihilation. Something happened at Nagasaki and Hiroshima which changed the whole background of life. The solidity of the world was once and for all destroyed. And there is not a doubt that that is at the back of the minds of many young people. Deep down there are three feelings, certainly inarticulate, perhaps even subconscious and un-realized, but certainly there—the feeling that their elders have betrayed them, the feeling that the Church has been tragically silent on the things that matter, and the feeling that in a situation like this what better can you do than eat, drink and be merry, for tomorrow we die? A situation like that could not but leave its mark on a generation which has known no other.

(iv) It is a tragically *short-sighted generation*. The tendency is to take the quick rewards. You have only to look at the dilemma of the professions today. Were it not for foreign doctors and nurses the Health Service would break down. The supply of teachers is desperately inadequate. No Church in the kingdom has an adequate supply of students

for its Ministry. Why? Because young people will seize the
quick reward and will refuse the four to seven years of
discipline which a profession demands. It is true that they
are on the way to an empty, unsatisfied, unrealized, boring
life; but they are nearly incapable of taking the long view of
things.

(v) It is a desperately *materialistic* generation. It is a
generation which can see no other reward than the financial
reward. It is an age which, as it has been said, knows the
price of everything and the value of nothing. There are few
who think in terms of anything else but pay, and there are
few who would ask for any particulars regarding a job except
the salary.

(vi) It is a generation which has to a very great extent *lost
its moral standards*. Promiscuity, illegitimacy, venereal
disease, broken marriages, are a commonplace.

And to make matters worse, there never was an age which
was continually subject to such constant moral attack. There
plays upon this generation a continual propaganda to vice.
One of the tragedies is that this generation chooses as its
objects of admiration the wrong people. It admires, for
instance, the film star who turns marriage into legalized
adultery. The influence of the public figures of the enter-
tainment world, with notable and splendid examples, is one
of the worst evils of this age. Further, the kind of thing
which is constantly shown on television, constantly shown on
posters, is so often a glorification of violence and a romanti-
cizing of immorality. It will be desperately difficult to get
back to the standards on which morality is built.

(vii) It is a generation which is likely to be *unfortunate in
the home*. There are so many of these young people who
come from broken homes, or from homes where there is an
armed neutrality instead of love. Even if that is not so, there
are so many homes in which children and parents have nothing to say to each other and are even uncomfortable in each

other's presence, homes in which a son or daughter is much more likely to take a problem to an admired teacher than a parent. There are far too many homes where the mother goes out to work. A television set, a motor-car, a new house, a continental holiday can cost too much. It is bad if there is no one to see the child off in the morning; it is worse if there is no one to welcome him home at night, and that in so many homes is the situation. The plain fact is that so many young people begin life with the cards stacked against them.

(viii) It is a generation which is peculiarly *ill-equipped to learn.* In many places the educational system is not far from having broken down; and there are classes of young people fifteen years old who have never in their lives been able even to attempt a written answer to any question and who never will. We have to teach and there never was a generation in a worse condition to be taught.

(ix) It is one of the most *destructive* generations in history. The amount of sheerly senseless destruction which goes on is almost unbelievable. A building in course of erection will be deliberately destroyed. Let a wood be near a certain kind of area and it will become a devastation. The explanation of this destructiveness is plain. It is given by the great psychologist Erich Fromm:

It would seem that the amount of destructiveness to be found in individuals is proportionate to the amount to which expansiveness of life is curtailed. . . . Life has an inner dynamic of its own; it tends to grow, to be expressed, to be loved. It seems that, if this tendency is thwarted, the energy directed towards life undergoes a process of decomposition and changes into energies directed towards destruction. . . . The more the drive towards life is thwarted, the stronger is the drive towards destruction. The more life is realized, the less is the strength of destructiveness. *Destructiveness is the outcome of unlived life.*

This is a destructive generation because by and large it has nothing to live for. It has never been educated in life.

(x) It remains to say that basically this generation has still two great qualities. It has *loyalty*, even if the only direction in which that loyalty is shown is to a gang or to a football team. It has *courage*, for it takes courage, for instance, to ride a motor-bicycle at a hundred miles an hour.

It is not that there is nothing left to appeal to—there is; but I do not think that the appeal has ever been purposely, deliberately and as a matter of policy made.

This is the group which I think it is not unfair to call the lost generation, and it is this group which constitutes our greatest challenge, and it is the group for which, with certain notable exceptions, neither the Church nor the YMCA has done very much. What is to be done?

(i) We must go out to them. I think that it may well be that the day of the big central YMCA institute or building is nearing an end. I think that the approach to this lost generation will fail unless clubs and institutes are set up in the new housing areas and the slum clearance schemes where they are mainly to be found. So often in these places they have nothing, not even a café, to take them off the streets. The YMCA could do not only a Christian service but also a social service by giving them some place near their homes which would be their own. It may well be that it would be far better to sell many of the great central buildings and use the money to go where youth is.

(ii) We must begin by establishing human contact with them. Human contact must be established long before religious contact is attempted. What is wanted in the initial stages is some place where we can meet them simply as human beings. To rush the religious side of the work would certainly be to ruin it. In the initial stages what is needed above all is a club where they can come and eat and dance and be together and where we can meet them as persons.

(iii) This will often involve a deliberate determination not to be shocked and the strength of will to disregard the complaints and the criticisms of the set who are shocked. It may well involve activities on the Sunday which the orthodox will abominate and the presentation of the Christian message in terms and in language which are new and strange.

The Church and the YMCA are always threatened by the same danger, the danger of becoming ingrowing, the danger of thinking of nothing but keeping things going as they are, the danger of being content to wait until people come in instead of going out to get them, and above all the danger of prolonging far too long the life of methods and approaches which in their day and generation have outlived their usefulness. Today the Church and the YMCA face a great choice. Are they to be outgoing or ingrowing? Choose ye this day whom ye will serve.

4

The Faith We Teach

WE might well call this the age of the demand for intel-
ligibility. There was a time when to be unintelligible was
the sign of a great preacher. There is a famous story of an
old woman who on leaving church was asked how she had
liked a sermon by Dr Norman Macleod, and who answered:
'God forbid that I should understand the great man.' That
kind of attitude is gone and gone for ever. Nowadays to be
listened to a man must be understood.

We may put that in another and far-reaching way.
Religion must always be contemporary; it must speak to a
man when and where he is and as he is; and, if that is so, the
language of religion must necessarily be contemporary. But
this means that right at the very beginning we are under a
twofold handicap.

(i) We are expounding a book which is written in Hebrew
and in Greek, the oldest parts of which were written about
900 BC and none of which is later than say AD 120. We are
expounding a book written in foreign languages, none of
which is nearer to us than almost 2,000 years ago. It is in the
thought-forms and the categories of thought and the meta-
phors of an ancient civilization quite unlike our own. I take
an example of the kind of thing that can happen. H. B.
Tristram in *Eastern Customs in Bible Lands* tells how once he
preached in Ceylon through an interpreter. As he later saw,
he very unfortunately chose as his subject the parable of the
lost sheep. Afterwards the interpreter said to him: 'Are

you aware, sir, that there is not a single person listening to you who has ever seen a sheep?' 'What did you do?' said Tristram. 'I turned it into a buffalo which had lost her calf,' the interpreter said, 'and who searched in the bush till she had found it.' Did it not ever strike you that the picture of the Good Shepherd is in fact quite strange to a city-born-and-bred child? Further, not only is the Bible ancient but it is most often read in a translation of it into Elizabethan English, English which no one has spoken for the last three hundred years and more. Somehow out of this situation the thing has to be made intelligible to 1966. The truth behind the ancient trappings has to be made contemporary.

(ii) Further, there has developed in the Church a kind of religious language.

If we are to convey the lesson of the faith to this generation, this jargon must be sternly set aside. The one essential rule will be never to utter a single sentence to which a definite and discernible meaning cannot be attached.

Let me take an example. Some short time ago I heard a vivid and emotionally moving sermon on the parable of the two builders. It finished with the sentence: 'If you build your life on Christ, you're safe! You're safe!' At the moment that is moving, but, when you allow yourself to stop feeling and to begin thinking, *what does it mean?* Safe from what? You are certainly not safe from temptation, not safe from death, not safe from sorrow, not safe from the slings and arrows of outrageous fortune, not safe from all the ills to which humanity is heir. What in the last analysis does this *mean?* Stop yourself over and over again with the demand, What does this mean? And, if you really can't tell, begin again. Nothing does religion more harm than the outpouring of fluent but meaningless pious jargon in what someone has called 'the language of Canaan'.

What then shall we teach?

(i) It is best to begin where we are, to begin with ourselves.

What are we to teach about *man*? *What is man*? There have been many definitions of man. Man has been called *a thinking animal*, for there is no other living creature which can look before and after. Man has been called *a tool-making animal*, for no other living creature makes and uses tools. Man has been called *a laughing animal* for laughter is confined to human beings. Man has been called *a cooking animal*, for of all living creatures he alone cooks his food.

The answer of the Bible is clear and unequivocal. Man is made in the image of God. That is to say, man is not an animal at all; man is kin to God.

As we see man just now, and as we know man ourselves, man is a mixture. As Studdert Kennedy said:

> *I'm a man and a man's a mixture*
> *Right down from his very birth,*
> *For part of him comes from heaven,*
> *And part of him comes from earth.*

Pictorially the Jews expressed that in the idea of the two angels; they said that beside every man there stood two angels, one a good angel beckoning him to goodness and nobility; the other an evil angel luring him downwards to sin and evil. More theologically the Jews expressed that in the doctrine of the two natures; they said that in every man there is the good nature and the evil nature warring against each other. Paul in Romans 7 painted the picture of himself tugged in two directions at the one time, able to see and to know and even to will the good thing, but quite unable to do it.

Man is made in the image of God; and yet man is this strange mixture, this permanently split personality. Clearly the one thing that is certainly true is, as it has been said, that whatever man is he is not what he was meant to be.

There is in life for any thinking person a feeling of helplessness. You see it in the international sphere; there is a

madness which may well end in the madness of war; every
ordinary person in the world wants to stop it—and nobody
can. There is in every one of us the desire for goodness; no
man is really satisfied with himself; we make our resolves and
our promises and our pledges—and nobody seems able to
keep them or to turn them into action.

What is the cause of this? The cause of this is sin. There
was a time when no one took sin very seriously; if you talked
about sin they listened with half an ear and went on doing
what they were doing. J. S. Whale quotes a paragraph from
T. L. Hulme: 'It is as if you pointed out to an old lady at a
garden party that there was an escaped lion twenty yards off,
and she were to reply, "Oh, yes," and then quietly take
another cucumber sandwich.' We are not now quite so easy-
going. Even the most thoughtless person can hardly help
seeing that there is something wrong with a world which is at
one and the same time in the grip of a moral rot which nothing seems able to stop and of a folly which may well end in
race suicide. It should not be difficult today to make anyone
see that something has gone wrong.

What then is sin? Sin, the worst thing in the world, comes
from the greatest gift which man possesses. It comes from
man's free will. In some way God created man with free
will. In all reverence we can only say that God had to. The
one thing that God wants from men is love, and without free
will there can be no such thing as love, for love must always
be the spontaneous uncoerced movement of the heart. But
man used his free will to take his own way of things. In one
sentence—*sin is thinking that you know better than God*.

Here then is the human situation and the human dilemma
from which we start. Man is made in the image of God; as
he is, man is a mixture; as he is, something has gone wrong;
that something is sin; and sin is basically the human pride
which thinks it is wiser than God.

(ii) Now we go on to ask, What do we believe about God?

It may well be that when we are trying to put into some teaching form what we believe about God and what we believe about Jesus, we shall find no better way to express our belief than in the terms of the great traditional and classical expressions of the Church's faith.

The great traditional expression of the faith sees God active in three spheres, in Creation, in Providence and in Redemption; they see God as Creator, Sustainer and Redeemer; and there is no better way in which to express the activity of God and his relationship to us and to his world.

(a) First, then, God is *Creator*. Now let us be clear straightaway that when we say that God is Creator we are not saying anything at all about the method by which God created the world. For long the early chapters of Genesis were a storm centre of biblical criticism. But they need not be so. If you are taking a class of young people, and if you are studying the first two chapters of the Bible, if you say to them: 'Can you put what these two chapters are saying into one sentence?', you will quite certainly get the answer: 'God created the world.' That is exactly and precisely what these chapters are saying. In reality they tell us nothing about the method by which God made the world; they were never intended to be parts of a text-book of *scientific* truth; they were from the beginning intended to be an affirmation and a witness of *spiritual* truth. They were intended to state the fact that life and the world have their beginning from God.

In point of fact modern knowledge has made the conception of creation infinitely greater and more thrilling. What science has shown is that God did not, as it were, create the world ready-made. God put life into the world, and allowed that life to develop. We can put it this way— and it is a very great thought—God allowed men to co-operate in the work of creation. What God did put into the world was life with a series of infinite possibilities and potentialities, and left it to men to work out, or to fail to

work out, the possibilities of life. God did not so much give
men life all ready-made and completed; He gave them the
raw materials of life; and challenged man to make life what
life ought to be.

So far from belittling the doctrine of creation it has made
it infinitely greater and more thrilling, for it has given us the
picture not so much of a God who made a series of things for
men as of a father who gives his children the immense
opportunity and privilege of making life for themselves.

We believe that God is Creator, and we believe that His
way of creating was to give man the opportunity of co-
operating in bringing to its reality God's own dream of what
the world should be.

(b) Second, God is *Sustainer*. We do not believe that God,
as it were, set things going and then left them alone. We
believe that God is still in the world which He has made.
Another way to put this would be that we believe that God is
still creating the world and still creating us.

There have been in the history of theological thought
three main ways of looking at the connection between God
and the world.

(i) There is the way of *pantheism*, which believes that God
is quite literally everything. We can cite as a rather crude but
illuminating example the belief of the Stoics. The Stoics
believed that God is what they called fiery spirit, far purer
and clearer than any earthly fire. They believed that the soul
of man is a spark, a *scintilla*, of that divine power and fire
which came to stay in a man's body. God thus dwells in
every man. But further, they believed that that fire became
what they called depotentiated, and that some of it became
dull and inert and that dull and inert material is the material
out of which everything in the world is made. According to
the Stoics God made everything, and out of God everything
is made. It is an extraordinary thought and it is a great
thought. It means that every single thing in this universe is

E

God. Man is a God-filled creature living in a God-filled universe. The Stoic went the whole way; in flies and dung-beetles and stones and trees and earth and air and sea there is God. It is plain to see that that is a noble creed, even if to some extent at least it shuts God up in his own universe. But it does inculcate a truth which cannot but awaken reverence for all men and all things, for all men and all things *are* God.

(ii) There is the way of *deism*, which is the very opposite of that. It conceives of God as being quite separate from and quite outside the world. God, as it were, made the world, but when He had made it He stepped aside from it and outside it. He may issue His commands; He may give His orders; He may even make His revelations, but He is not involved in the world. He is apart from the world. He may watch it and He may judge it, but He is not actually in it. This would certainly give us a picture of a God whom we could worship and adore, but not the picture of a God whom we can meet in intimate loving fellowship.

To these two ways of belief special names have been given. Pantheism stresses the *immanence* of God, the fact that God is and dwells in everything. Deism stresses the *transcendence* of God, the fact that God is high and lifted up, the Holy One, apart and distant from and above the world, splendid, magnificent, and majestic, but not in life.

(iii) There is the way of *theism*. Theism takes these two ways of thought and combines them. It holds that God did make the world and is not identified with the world; but that none the less God is still in the world, controlling, directing, revealing Himself to, pleading with, men. This is the Christian belief. The Christian does not doubt the fact that God is holy and that God is God, different from man in being and essence; but the Christian also believes in the Providence of God. He believes that God is working all things together for good; he believes that there is a purpose and a plan; he believes that God is closer to us than breathing and nearer than hands or feet; and he believes—and here we are back at the basic definition of sin—that the tragedy of life is that man with the terrible responsibility of free-will can reject and refuse this loving care of God.

(c) So then we believe that God is creator and sustainer; but still further we believe that God is _Redeemer_.

This means the further involvement of God in the world. To put it in a very human way—God is a person. Now the very essence of personality is that it finds its fulfilment and its satisfaction in relationships with other persons. A person cannot develop himself alone; he needs the love, the friendship, the interaction, the relationship with other persons. That is precisely why friendlessness and loneliness are so very difficult to bear. Now if God is a person, then God _needs_ other persons; God, too, we can say in all reverence, needs to be known and loved. We can therefore say that for God _the creation of the world was a divine necessity_. He had to have people to know Him and to love Him and to enter into a relationship with Him. But—again to put the matter in a very human way—when God created the world He created nothing but heartbreak for Himself; He created nothing but trouble. In view of that situation God could do three things. He could simply abandon the world to its fate and to its devices. He could be like a parent who decides that there is nothing to be done. He could simply in anger and judgement wipe out the world; He could with his divine _fiat_ destroy the world which was giving Him so much trouble. Or, God could seek to find some way to mend the situation and to bring men back to Himself.

Here is the essence of Christian belief. God neither abandoned the world, nor destroyed the world. In some way in Jesus Christ He entered into the world to bring men back to Himself, to make men accept Him instead of rejecting Him, to make men submit to Him instead of rebelling against Him, to make men love Him instead of disregarding Him or hating Him. To put it quite simply, God in Jesus Christ pleads with men to come back to Himself and shows them the way to come back.

So then we must teach that God is Creator, Redeemer and Sustainer of the world.

(iii) This brings us directly to two things; it brings us directly to the Christian view of the *world*, and to the Christian view of *Jesus Christ*. First, then, let us look at the Christian view of the world.

We must always carefully remember that the Christian does not despise the world. In the ancient world there were those—and the belief has never wholly died—who held that the world is essentially bad. In particular there were the Gnostics. The Gnostics were faced—as we are all faced—with the problem of sin, and suffering and sorrow. Their explanation was twofold. They believed that matter was as old as God, that from the beginning there were, so to speak, two realities in the world, matter and God. They further believed that the whole trouble is due to the fact that this always existing matter had and has an essential flaw in it, that it is bad material. Therefore anything that is made out of it is necessarily bad. They further believed that the true God could not possibly touch this evil matter, and that therefore creation is the work of a lesser God, ignorant of and hostile to the real and true God. The necessary consequence of a belief like that is that the world is evil, that it never can be good, that it is doomed to destruction, that the body is bad, and that therefore the duty of the true man is to withdraw himself from the world as completely and totally as he can.

There always have been those who sang that earth is a desert drear; there always have been those who were quite frankly suspicious of everything in the world; there always have been those who have suspected the body and who have regarded sex as an evil thing; there always have been those who, to put it quite generally, have regarded it as a sin to enjoy the world. Let us be quite clear that that is actually a heresy and quite unchristian.

But Christianity does not swing to the opposite direction. It does not proceed to say that everything in the garden is lovely, and that all is for the best in the best of all possible worlds. One of the most significant things that Jesus ever did was to teach us to pray: 'Thy kingdom come; Thy will be done in earth as it is in heaven.' Clearly Jesus believed that you can build the kingdom on earth; that on earth there can arise a society in which God's will is as perfectly done as it is in heaven. Now what that means is that what is really important is, not what the world is, but what the world can become; not the *actuality* but the *potentiality* of the world. From this we can and must draw two conclusions.

(*a*) We are bound to believe that this is essentially a friendly universe. Lessing said that if he had one question to ask the Sphinx it would be: 'Is this a friendly universe?' Dick Sheppard tells of a time when he was out on the Downs on a dark night and when he seemed to feel close to him, around him and about him, the spirit of the universe, and when he had one almost overmastering desire, to shout out: 'Friend or foe?' There are times when every man feels that life is a conspiracy to break us. Illness, pain, sorrow, suffering, things beyond explanation, things which leave you with a pain-wracked body or a broken heart—these things come, and sometimes we have the feeling that life is out to smash us. But the Christian view of the world is that no matter how sore things may be, no matter how inexplicable they may be, essentially and basically this is a friendly universe. In any situation we have to ask George Carver's question: 'Mr Creator, what do you want me to do?' and we have to ask: 'What is God meaning me and the world to make out of this situation?' There will be times in life when nothing matters nearly so much as to hang on to that conviction. As Robert Louis Stevenson said: 'I believe in the love of God and if I woke up in hell I would still believe in it.' Or as Job said: 'Though he slay me, yet will I trust him.'

(b) But out of this there comes something which is not so much comfort as challenge. If the importance of the world lies in the potential of the world, if, to put it in another way, the world is a dream of God, then there is laid upon us the duty of seeking to realize that potential. It is through us that the potential must be realized; it is through us that the dream must come true; in other words, as Paul has it, *we are fellow-labourers with God*. The world for us becomes a place in which the supreme duty of man is to enable God to realize His purposes for the world.

We must teach that the world is not evil; we must teach that the supreme fact about the world is that in it it has the potential of the kingdom of God; we must therefore teach that in the realest sense all things are intended to work together for good; and we must teach that therefore there is laid on us the supreme duty and the supreme privilege of being fellow-workers with God.

(iv) This then brings us inevitably to our belief in *Jesus Christ*. When we were thinking about God, we saw that the classical and traditional titles of God gave us exactly the line we needed. We will find the same with regard to Jesus Christ. The traditional titles of Jesus are *Prophet*, *Priest*, and *King*. Let us then look at Jesus in these three capacities.

(a) Jesus is *Prophet*. What does that mean for us? We find the very essence of the function and the person of the prophet in the great saying of Amos (3[7]): 'God will do nothing without revealing it to his servants the prophets.' A Prophet is a man who is within the confidence and the counsels of God. The whole idea of a prophet has suffered and been belittled by the insistent connection of the prophet with the idea of foretelling the future. The prophet is far more a *forth-teller* than a *foreteller*; his function is far more to forthtell the will of God than to foretell the future. The prophet is the voice of God to men. He has stood in the counsels of God; he knows the will of God; he has the courage to speak to men without fear and without favour; what God has said he will speak.

Of Jesus this is supremely true. Jesus is the Prophet; and, when we hear Jesus speak, we can say: 'This is the voice of God.'

This may be put in another way. Jesus is the supreme *Revealer* of God. When we look at Jesus, we can say: 'This is how God acts.' When we hear Him speak we can say: 'This is the voice of God.'

(b) Jesus is *Priest*. For many people nowadays the word 'priest' has an unpleasant sound; but essentially the function of the priest is a great function. We get it best of all in the Latin word for 'priest' which is '*pontifex*', and '*pontifex*' means a bridge-builder. The Priest is the one who builds a bridge between God and man. Here is the very essence of the work of Jesus; he builds a bridge between God and man. He brings together man and God. We will not stop to argue how He does that. There are those who see His work in terms of sacrifice and who hold that He made the sacrifice which atones for the sin of man. There are those who see His work in terms of such a demonstration of the love of God that all our fear and terror and estrangement are taken away, and we cannot help, as it were, casting ourselves into the arms of the God who loved us like that. How we explain it is not important; what is important is that in Jesus we see the One who at the cost of His life and His death opened the way for man to God. He enables us to be, to put it very simply, friends with God.

(c) Jesus is *King*. This right at the beginning involves something. It involves the conviction that *Jesus is still alive*. To say He is *Prophet*, and to say He is *Priest*, is to say something about what He *did*: to say He is *King* is to say something of what He is. Jesus is not a figure in a book; He is a living presence. He is not someone about whom we learn; He is someone whom we experience.

The Christian lives in a continual Easter Day; Sunday is for him the day which in historical fact commemorates his Risen Lord. That which differentiates Jesus from all the great figures of the past is the simple and basic fact that He is not past; He is present.

But to say that He is King means that He claims as a right our obedience. It is not enough to be interested in Him; we must be committed to Him. It is not enough to discuss Him; we must follow Him.

We have to present Jesus as the one who spoke the last word about God and about life; and to whom we must give an obedience and a loyalty which nothing can shake.

(v) We have thought about ourselves and our world and about Jesus and God. This leads our thoughts inevitably to that one great gift which establishes and maintains contact between man and God, between us and Jesus Christ. That is the gift of *prayer*; in our teaching it is essential that we should teach the true way of prayer. The tragedy of the situation in regard to prayer is that there are so many who have abandoned it or to whom it is a mere formality, because quite frankly they have come to the conclusion that prayer does not work. It may well be said that there is more wrong teaching both in words and in implications about prayer than about almost anything in the Christian life. There is a technique of everything and there is a technique of prayer. It is perfectly possible for a man to possess something of the greatest value and yet to fail to get the most out of it and to make the most of it because he is not using it in the right way. There are certain laws of prayer which must never be forgotten.

(a) First and foremost, there is nothing so essential in prayer as honesty and sincerity. Luther always said that the first law of prayer is: 'Don't lie to God.' We often hear prayers in conventional biblical language, especially from the Psalms, which may have been quite honest on the lips of David but which are mere formalities on our lips. The plain truth is that we often say things in prayer which we quite certainly do not mean and we often ask for things which we have not the slightest expectation of receiving, and which in fact we do not wish to receive. Augustine was the greatest Christian thinker after Paul. In his young days he lived anything but a good life. But he had the experience which so many have had; when he was good he wanted to be bad, and when he was bad he wanted to be good. He could not really be happy either way. And he tells us in his *Confessions* that he used to kneel down and pray: 'O God, make me pure, make me pure,' and then he would add in a whisper, 'but not yet, but not yet.' Augustine was at least honest enough to admit that he did not really want his prayer to be answered. We often pray to be changed and the last thing we really want is to be changed. We sing in prayer to God:

> *Were the whole realm of nature mine,*
> *That were an offering far too small;*
> *Love so amazing, so divine,*
> *Demands my life, my soul, my all—*

and all the chances are that if the Church asked from us an extra five shillings a week—which is about the same as the price of a packet of cigarettes—we would either point-blank refuse it or we would think it far too much.

Prayer demands honest self-examination as a primary basis. When we pray we must be asking all the time, 'Do I really mean this?' And we must see to it that we are not using empty words to God who knows the secrets of the heart.

(b) We must never forget that prayer means a co-operative effort between us and God. No sooner have we prayed than we must set out to make our own prayers come true. There is no point in a student praying to pass an examination if he has done none of the work. There is no good in praying for health if we deliberately do the things which a doctor forbids us to do. There is no good in praying that God's kingdom may come and that the heathen may be converted if we are not prepared to give a penny to help the work. There is no point in praying that the lonely may be cheered and the sorrowing comforted unless we are prepared to do something for the lonely and the sorrowful ones in our own congregation and street.

It must always be remembered that prayer is not an easy way of getting things without any effort on our part; it is not pushing all the work off on to God. God does not begin to help us until we begin to help ourselves. Prayer is not us doing it and it is not God doing it, it is us and God doing it together.

(c) It must be remembered that prayer does not disturb natural laws. However good a Christian a man was and however sincerely he prayed, if he fell out the window of the fortieth floor of a skyscraper it would not stop him falling until he reached the ground. That man is in the grip of the law of gravity which is not to be broken.

Here is where the damage is done. It is for instance possible that a teacher may pray for good weather for an excursion or outing. Such prayer will make not the slightest difference, and in any case when we are praying for sunshine the farmer might well be praying for rain. To pray like that is to present young people with a wrong view of prayer from the beginning. Of course, prayer like that does not work. The correct prayer in such a case is that we should be enabled to enjoy ourselves, hail, rain or shine.

Here is the very essence of the point. Prayer is not escape; prayer is conquest. Prayer does not release a man from a situation; it enables him to go through it in victory. Jesus was not saved from the Cross; He was enabled to accept the Cross triumphantly.

It may well be that the wrongest thing of all in the attitude of so many people to prayer is that they try to use prayer as a means of escaping things, of running away from things, whereas prayer is a means of triumphantly facing the unfaceable and doing the undoable and bearing the unbearable and passing the breaking-point without breaking.

(d) Lastly, there are too many people who think of prayer almost entirely in terms of talking and with almost no idea of listening. In real prayer we listen even more than we speak. Prayer is not us telling God; it is God telling us. Prayer is not us telling God what we want Him to do; it is at least as much God telling us what He wants us to do. It is us saying to God: 'Lord, what do you want me to do?' But so many of us in our prayers never even give God the chance to speak. In prayer there should be at least as much of silence as of speech.

We have to try to teach young people how to pray.

(vi) Last of all, we have to teach that this life is not the end. The belief in a life to come is an integral and essential part of the Christian faith.

In an Irish play there is a picture of the days of the famines. Sometimes in those days simply to give them a pay men were set to digging roads that were not of the slightest use whatsoever. In the play a young man discovers what is going on and comes into his father, broken in heart and in spirit. 'They're digging roads,' he says, 'that lead to nowhere.' It is an essential part of the Christian faith that life is not a road that leads to nowhere; it is a road that leads to God; and the tremendous importance of this life is that it is the training-ground for eternity.

Here then is the faith we teach. We want to produce young people who are—

conscious of the human dilemma;

continuously aware of God as their Creator, Sustainer and Redeemer;

with a vivid sense of the responsibility of life, and of the
privilege of being the co-workers of God;

certain of the unique lordship of Jesus Christ;

with a real knowledge of the meaning of prayer;

and always mindful of the life beyond the horizons of time.

5

The Methods of Our Teaching

THERE is much more to teaching than having an intellectual, academic, technical knowledge of the subject involved, although, of course, such knowledge is a basic prerequisite. But it always remains true that a first-class honours degree in any subject is no guarantee that a man can teach it. There is much more to teaching than expertness in the technique of teaching and in teaching-methods, although it is true that a man can waste an enormous amount of knowledge because he does not know the technique of communicating it. Knowledge is necessary, technique is necessary; but these are, so to speak, the skeleton of the subject and they have still to be clothed with living flesh. A man with a wide fund of knowledge and with a mastery of technique is like a perfectly laid fire to which someone has still to set a match, if it is to warm the room.

There are certain great truths which we must realize and never forget if we are to teach in any sense of the term at all. Some of these things sound like platitudes. None the less they must be stated, if the foundation is to be laid.

(1) We must realize the sheer *importance* of the task. The Jews had a saying that a man who taught a child the law had been honoured with as great a privilege as Moses himself who received the law from the hands of God. The Jews had a saying: 'Dearer to me is the breath of school children than the savour of sacrifices.' It is obvious that teaching must be done, if every generation is not to enter upon life naked and

unequipped for the task of living. It is our privilege to have received the truth; it is our responsibility to transmit the truth.

Sometimes in the early Church we come across the body of men known as teachers. Paul, writing to the Corinthians, says:

God has appointed in the Church first apostles, second prophets, third teachers (I Corinthians 12^{28}).

The teachers are ranked with the prophets and the apostles. He writes to the Ephesians of the gifts of God:

And His gifts were that some should become apostles, some prophets, some evangelists, some pastors and teachers for the equipment of the saints, for the work of the ministry, for the building up of the body of Christ (Ephesians 4$^{11-12}$).

It was the prophets and teachers of the Church at Antioch who sent out Paul and Barnabas on that first missionary journey by which the whole history of the world was changed (Acts 13^1).

In the days of the early Church there were, of course, very few books, and such books as there were were in price far beyond the ability of the ordinary man to buy. So when a man entered the Church he was handed over to the teachers for instruction. Long before the Church possessed a written gospel at all the teachers were the living books, the repositories of the Christian story and the Christian truth, which it was their duty to pass on to others. The early Church could not have existed, and Christianity could not have spread, without the teachers.

The situation today is not essentially different. In the early days of the Church there was an old collector of knowledge called Papias to whom we still owe much of our knowledge of how the gospels came to be written. He tells us that in his search for truth he preferred to all books 'the living and abiding voice'. Truth will always be more effectively communicated by the living voice than by the printed page.

It is certainly not too much to say that in the Church and in the community there is no more important task than teaching.

(2) We must realize the *responsibility* of the task. The more precious the material, the greater the responsibility of the man who has to work with it. When material is such that a mistake cannot be unmade then the responsibility becomes even greater. The material with which the teacher works is the human mind. We have already quoted Ignatius' well-known saying: 'Give me a child for the first seven years of his life, and I care not who gets him afterwards.' If this saying is true positively, it is equally true negatively. If early teaching can stamp a young mind for goodness and for truth, then equally it can injure and hurt that same mind. The mind is plastic and will take every single impression that is made upon it. In point of physical fact that part of the brain with which we think and remember is the colour and the consistency of tooth paste. If we think a thought once it leaves a microscopic scratch on it; if we think the thought twice the scratch becomes deeper; if we go on thinking that thought the scratch becomes a groove and the thoughts will not come out of it. The thought will travel in it like the wheel of a car inextricably caught in a deep cart-rut on a country road.

It is also true that we literally never forget anything. Memory works, as it were, in three stages. There are those things which are on the surface of the memory and which are immediately accessible; there are those things which are as it were beneath a screen just below the surface, and by a conscious effort these things can be recalled to the memory. And there are those things which lie beneath the surface altogether, in the subconscious part of the memory. They may never be consciously remembered; it may be impossible deliberately to bring them to the surface unless under the influence of hypnotism or drugs; but they are there. A classic example of that is the case of the servant girl who was ill and whose mind was wandering. She appeared to be reciting long stretches of something which at first no one could understand. Then someone discovered that what she was reciting was in fact whole chapters of the Old Testament in Hebrew, not a word of which she, of course, consciously knew. The reason was that she had at one time been employed in a minister's house. This minister had had the habit of walking up and down his study reading the Hebrew Bible aloud. When he was doing this the girl had been scrubbing the landing-floor outside his study door. She had heard; what she had heard had lodged, as everything does, in her subconscious mind and now it was released by her illness and was coming out.

The teacher marks the plastic mind of the young person indelibly for good or for evil.

Herein lies the awe-inspiring responsibility of teaching. All great leaders have been moved and even haunted by this sense of responsibility. During the war there were two great leaders. General Montgomery, as he then was, used to say that his one daily prayer was that 'I may not be allowed to fail my men'. It is told that Eisenhower was taking the salute of the march-past at Tripoli after the North African victory. First there came the Free French, battle-scarred and almost in rags. Next there came the Americans, great technical troops but without the last word in military precision. Then there came the Brigade of Guards. It is said that at that moment Eisenhower turned to Alexander who was on the dais beside him. 'Who am I,' he said, 'to command men like these?'

To the end of the day the teacher must have this colossal sense of the responsibility of his task. The man who approaches teaching lightly will not be without his own judgement in the sight of God.

(3) The teacher must have *a vivid and continual awareness*

of the potential of those whom he teaches. It is the simple truth
that no teacher knows what any child or young person in his
class may become, and therefore in the most literal sense, no
teacher knows what he is doing.

It is told that an old German teacher used to take off his
hat and bow to his class every time he met them first thing in
the morning. When he was asked why, his answer was: 'You
never know what one of these boys may become.' And he
was right—for there was a little lad in that class called Martin
Luther. When Duke Robert of Burgundy set out for the
wars, he knew that he might not come back and he wished to
see that the succession to the throne was safe. So he brought
his little baby son, not more than a few months old, and he
made his lords and earls and barons swear fealty to the baby.
As one of his nobles knelt before the child, and as he took
the oath, he smiled. 'What are you smiling at?' Duke Robert
asked. 'The baby is so little,' said the noble. 'True,' said
Duke Robert. 'He's little, but he'll grow.' He did—that
child became William the Conqueror, the first Norman king
of England.

There is something which it is very lovely, very moving,
and very inspiring to remember. Jesus must have attended
the village school of Nazareth, for Jesus too grew in wisdom
and in stature. He must have learned to read and write and
count, and to acquire the basic skills and information which
every boy needs to make a living. The name of that teacher
we do not know, and we shall never know it—but what a teacher
he must have been and what a potential he had in his class!

In every class of young people and in every group of young
men there is an explosive dynamic which can alter history
and change the world.

In all teaching we must begin by being vividly and consistently aware of the importance of our task, of the responsibility of our task, and of the tremendous potential of the
young people we teach.

F

From this, one obligation obviously and inevitably follows:
*The teacher must never teach without the most careful and con-
scientious preparation.* If the task is of such awe-inspiring
importance, then to approach it unprepared is nothing less
than sin.

There is a kind of teacher and preacher who will begin a
talk, a lesson, or a sermon by saying: 'As I was coming down
the road I was wondering what I would speak to you about
and I saw . . .' Any class or audience would be perfectly
justified in rising in a body and walking out, when any man
begins his approach to them with an insult like that.

Of the Bible this fact is specially true. The Bible is a
difficult book; it is written in foreign languages; it comes
from an ancient civilization, the whole background of which
is quite different from that in which we live; it thinks in the
categories and the thought forms of its day and generation,
and they are not ours. To teach it, to make it relevant, and
intelligible, requires the most careful preparation.

Let me admit quite frankly that there is a great temptation
here. When one has been preaching and teaching for a long
time, there is an almost overwhelming temptation not to
bother preparing what one thinks one knows. Everything
will be all right. Preparation is not necessary. My chief
was G. H. C. Macgregor, one of the greatest New Testament
scholars in the world. He held his chair in Glasgow for
thirty years, and before that he held a chair in America; but
he once told me that the last thing he did every night before
he went to bed was to take out the next day's lectures and go
over them in every detail. You would not think he needed to
do so; he thought he did.

Work at your teaching; it pays dividends; it makes your
teaching live. Above all work at the discovery of facts. Facts
are the most interesting things in the world; there is hardly
an audience which cannot be captured by interesting facts
interestingly presented. But facts do not present themselves

facts have to be discovered and learned. Let us illustrate by taking three facts, one from geography, one from linguistics, and one from background customs in the New Testament.

(a) Few people realize the smallness of Palestine. Palestine is about 140 miles from north to south and less than fifty miles from east to west. This is to say that it is considerably farther from London to Eastbourne or Brighton than it is across the whole of Palestine; the whole width of Palestine is about the same as the distance between Glasgow and Edinburgh. It is literally possible to see from one end of Palestine to the other. Mount Hermon can be seen in the extreme north from the depression of the Dead Sea basin in the extreme south. It is very nearly twice as far from York to London as it is from the north to south of Palestine. Further, at its largest the population of Palestine never exceeded 4,000,000 people. The whole hopes of the Jewish nation and the whole history of Christianity have to be read in the light of the fact that they came from this incredibly small country and nation.

(b) The Beatitude says: 'Blessed are the meek.' Meek is not a word which is likely to have any appeal to a healthy minded teenager. Let us look at the word; the word is *praus*; and it is discussed at length by Aristotle. Aristotle described every virtue in terms of the mean, or of what we would call the happy medium. On the one side there was excess; on the other side there was defect; and in between there was the thing in its true and proper proportion. So on the one hand, the side of excess, there is the reckless man; on the other side, the side of defect, there is the cowardly man; and in between in the happy medium there is the brave man. Now Aristotle describes the quality which *praus* describes as the happy medium between too much and too little anger; it describes the man who stands in the medium position between the man who is too angry and the man who is never angry at all. It describes the man who is angry at the right people, for the right length of time, and for the right reason. So then, 'Blessed are the meek', means 'Blessed is the man who is always angry at the right time and never angry at the wrong time'. And that indeed is meaningful for the teenager of 1966.

(c) It is the command of Jesus that, 'If anyone strikes you on the right cheek, turn to him the other also'. For many this is a kind of one-sentence summary of Christianity. But what does it mean? To strike a man on the cheek is to slap him across the face. A slap, if it is given with force, is given with the palm of the hand. It is possible and natural to slap a man on the *left* cheek in that way; but if you are to slap him on the right cheek, you must either contort the hand in such a way that no force can be exerted; or you must flick him on the cheek with the back of the hand. Now in Jewish codified law a flick with the back of the hand is a far worse insult than an honest blow, and is punishable with double damages. What this therefore means is: No matter how bitterly and contemptuously and deliberately a man insults you, you must never resent it and grow bitter about it. Now if Christianity meant turning the other cheek when we are slapped, we would get very little opportunity to practise it; but if Christianity means refusing to resent insults and slights, we get the opportunity to practise it every day.

The truth is that the Holy Spirit helps those who help themselves, but the Holy Spirit cannot instruct us in the illuminating facts which interpret Scripture unless we are prepared to work ourselves. The man who will not study has automatically deprived himself of the help of the Holy Spirit, but the man who will study will be helped mightily. In the ancient days the Holy Spirit was operative in the writing of Scripture; in modern days the Holy Spirit is operative in the interpretation of Scripture, when we give our minds to it. The thing has been summed up in the sentence of advice: 'Prepare as if there were no such person as the Holy Spirit; preach as if there were no one but the Holy Spirit.'

The teacher must work; when he works the Holy Spirit works with him—but not unless.

We must next note another basic fact. *All success in teaching comes from certain attitudes to those who are taught.* Before a man can teach he must feel towards those whom he does teach in a certain way or ways. There is an unseen but a very real link between teacher and taught, and it will be quite clear to those who are taught whether these attitudes are present or not.

(i) First and foremost, the teacher must *respect* those whom he teaches. He must be quite clear that those whom he teaches have independent personalities and minds—and that they have every right to have them. The fact that we seek to teach those who are independent thinking personalities provides us with the fundamental and essential aim of all teaching. It is of the first importance to remember that we are not trying to persuade people to think as we think; we are trying to persuade people to think for themselves. Dostoevsky the great Russian novelist gave certain advice to young people: 'Talk nonsense, but your own nonsense. To go wrong in one's own way is better than to go right in some one else's.'

A modern writer of detective novels may seem a strange person from whom to take an illustration in theology. In Agatha Christie's detective stories there appear Hercule Poirot, the famous Belgian detective, and Captain Hastings, the simple soul who plays Watson to Poirot's Sherlock Holmes. In one story Hastings says to Poirot: 'I've learned a good deal from you one way or another.' Poirot's reply is: 'No human being should learn from another; each individual should develop his own power to the utmost, not try to imitate those of someone else. I do not wish you to be a second and inferior Poirot: I wish you to be the supreme Hastings.'

There is no worse teaching in this world than the teaching which produces a copy of the teacher; there is no worse teacher in this world than the teacher who so impresses his personality on the person taught that the personality of the person taught is obliterated.

Jesus knew this. At Caesarea Philippi he asked His disciples: 'Who do men say that I am?' They told Him that some thought Him to be Jeremiah, others Elijah, others one of the prophets, still others John the Baptist brought back to life. I think that there was a pause, then comes the one essential question: 'Who do *you* say that I am?'

Here is the very essence of Jesus's teaching method. Jesus's great teaching instrument was the parable. The one essential characteristic of the parable as a teaching instrument is that it compels a man to discover truth for himself. It does not tell him the truth. It says: 'Look, here is a story from which you ought to be able to deduce something. Listen to it, and then tell me what you think.' Here is truth—if you have eyes to see it. Here is truth—if you will make the effort to discover it yourself.

The plain truth of teaching is that the good teacher knows quite well that he has to be prepared to allow the pupil to go wrong. I often wonder if one of the lessons of the parable of the Prodigal Son might be startling if stated as, 'Every man has a right to his own sins'. I have always thought that one of the quite extraordinary features of that parable is the fact that *the father made not the slightest attempt to stop the son going off into the far country*. It was as if he was saying: 'Well, you will have to learn your own way; for that is the only way in which you will ever learn.'

The teacher has to be prepared that his pupil should become a heretic. Very recently I was away at a weekend conference with certain young people. I discovered that one of the complaints they had against the Church was, 'The Church doesn't trust us'. There is many a teacher who does not trust his pupils to think and who wants to do their thinking for them. A very short time ago I was lunching with a famous scientist. He is a very Christian man and spends much of his time serving the Church, specially in youth groups. He was saying that recently he had been with a youth group; he had spoken; the discussion was on; to use his own word, they dissected him, and were busy probing and questioning and enquiring and contradicting without mercy. Then the minister of the Church arrived; and, said this scientist, from that moment all the adventure went out of the discussion and it became flat and conventional and boringly orthodox. W. M. Macgregor said of A. B. Bruce the great Scottish teacher and theologian: 'He cut the cables and gave us a glimpse of the blue water.' I suppose that one of the first essentials of a good teacher is simply never to be shocked. It was said of the Greeks that they believed that there was no question which it was wrong to ask, and that they believed that in the end even God Himself must stand and deliver.

The teacher must remember that it is not his duty to teach the young person either to think or to speak as he does; it is his duty to teach him to think. And if the resulting thoughts should be strange thoughts then the teacher must have enough respect for the young person to let him go his own way in the confidence that he will finish up in the right place in the end—if he thinks hard enough, and long enough, and independently enough.

(ii) Second, and even more important, the teacher must *love* the person he teaches. There is more than one possible attitude to the person who is being taught. There is the attitude of *domination*, the wrongness of which we have just been seeing. A novelist makes one of the characters say to a child: 'I'll beat the fear of the loving God into you.' The teacher may rule by fear, either the fear of actual physical violence, or, what is perhaps worse, the fear of a bitter and sarcastic tongue. There is the attitude of *tolerance*. There are teachers who tolerate their pupils as a necessary evil. There is the attitude of *superior contempt*. As Carlyle said: 'There are twenty-seven and a half million people in this country— mostly fools.' There is the attitude which quite plainly looks on the person to be taught as a *nuisance*. But there is Jesus's attitude of *love*. The attitude of Jesus was love. As Mark tells the story of the Rich Young Ruler, there comes the lovely and revealing phrase: 'And Jesus, looking at him, loved him.' There is the attitude of Jesus and of the disciples to the children who were brought to Jesus. The disciples did their best to chase the children away. Jesus said: 'Let them come to me; don't try to stop them.' The important thing about that incident is not the incident in itself; it is *when it happened*. It happened when Jesus was on his last journey to Jerusalem. The tension of his soul was visible in the very look on his face. The action of the disciples was not due to any dislike of children; it was simply that at that terrible and crucial time they wished to protect Jesus; they did not want him troubled and bothered. And yet even at a time like that Jesus wanted them there.

An attitude is quite intangible; but an attitude is perfectly recognizable; and above all it is intensely feelable. Let us put two things side by side. Richard Church tells of his first going to school after the warm loving atmosphere of his own home. He says there was a feeling of 'cold, impersonal benevolence'. On the other hand it was said by one of her pupils of that great teacher, Alice Freeman Palmer: 'She makes you feel as if you were bathed in sunshine.'

Teaching is based on the conviction that people are more important than anything else in the world. One of the great American educationists was Kermit Eby. In spite of the fact that he was principal of a great school, with a vast burden of teaching and administration, the door of his study was continuously open for any of his scholars to come in. When he was asked how he bore the constant interruptions, his answer was: 'People are always more important than footnotes.'

It is quite fatal to regard any young person as a specimen of this or that type. It is still more fatal to regard any young person as a problem to be solved. Anyone in this world is a person to be loved—and therein lies the very basis of teaching.

(iii) This attitude of respect warmed by love will beget the three utter necessities of teaching.

(a) It will beget *encouragement*. In the Royal Navy there is a regulation in Queen's Regulations: No officer shall speak discouragingly to any other officer in the performance of his duties. An ounce of praise is worth a ton of criticism.

(b) It will beget *sympathy*. So often what people need in this world almost more than anything else is to be understood. The greatest claim of any teacher was the claim of Ezekiel: 'I sat where they sat.' To think and feel with the person taught is the way to teach.

(c) It will beget *patience*. The Jews had a saying: 'An irritable man cannot teach.' One of the dangers of teaching is the failure to see how the other person finds it all so difficult. The teacher needs something of the patience of God with the unteachability of men.

In view of all this, what then shall be our aims in teaching? What are we trying to do? How shall we define our objective? The experts in teaching say that we ought to aim to give those taught three things.

(i) We ought to try to give them *something to feel*. The supreme danger of both preaching and teaching is that it may be boring. The problem is that people can teach and people can listen to the most tremendous things with a kind of placid and lethargic indifference. One thing is quite certain. No man can teach with a cold heart; and no man can teach without some appeal to the emotions.

Especially in the teaching of the Christian truth the first

essential is to give the impression that this thing matters; and if it is clear that it matters intensely to the teacher there is some hope of it mattering to the person to be taught. A short time ago I was in a group of ministers who were celebrating the twenty-fifth anniversary of their ordinations. Naturally there were reminiscences. We were remembering our old teachers. In those days there was a Professor of Hebrew called W. B. Stevenson, who was one of the world's experts in Hebrew, but usually quite above the heads of the students he taught. One of the men remembering said: 'You remember old Stevenson. Sometimes he would get all excited about some point of Hebrew grammar or syntax, or some abstruse point of translation. None of us had more than the faintest glimmering of what he was talking about and most of us hadn't even that; but we did have the conviction that there must be something worth getting excited about.' More than half the problem of teaching lies, not in the communication of knowledge, but in the communication of enthusiasm. That is so often where we abjectly and miserably fail.

Rhadakrishnan, the great Indian poet and thinker, once said of the western teachers: 'Your theologians seem to me like men talking in their sleep.' J. S. Whale said that the trouble was that we sit around with our feet on the mantelpiece and pipe in mouth talking about theories of the Atonement instead of bowing down before the wounds of Christ; that we scurry about the burning bush, taking photographs from suitable angles instead of taking our shoes from off our feet, because the place wherein we stand is holy ground.

Florence Barclay, the once-famous author of *The Rosary*, tells how she was taken for the first time to Church, as it happened, to the Good Friday service. At first she played with the bibles and the books and the hassocks. Then there came the long Good Friday lesson; the minister read it superbly; the story gripped the child. She heard Judas betray and Peter deny; she heard the High Priest's bullying questions; she heard the long interview with Pilate and heard Pilate sway hither and thither. Something must happen, this lovely figure must not be killed. The rest of the congregation were sitting placidly unmoved. To the child it was stark tragedy; and then there came the words with a terrible finality:

Then delivered he him therefore unto them to be crucified, and they took Jesus and led him away and he bearing his cross went forth to a place that is called the place of a skull, which is called in the Hebrew tongue Golgotha.

And then there came the tragic words: 'where they crucified him.'

And suddenly the child sank down in the pew weeping as if her heart would break: 'Why did they do it, mother, why did they do it?' her grief-stricken childish voice rang through the church.

Here is the feeling which must and can be awakened. It is the tragedy that Churches are inextricably connected with weary boredom. The fault is ours so often; we even read the Bible with no thrill in the voice, as if it were a passage from a railway time-table.

We are so often half-bored with our teaching and inevitably those who listen are totally bored.

Something to feel is an essential of teaching; and you can't give anyone something to feel which you don't feel yourself.

(ii) But you cannot leave the matter there; to leave the matter there would be to wrap it up in a kind of golden haze. No doubt the matter must begin by wakening interest through this feeling, but that cannot be the end. The very same J. S. Whale who spoke about the danger of sitting around talking about theories says in another part of the same book:

Christian testimony which raises no questions for the heart does raise them for thought. They may be insoluble, but not to tackle them would mean theological suicide.

This is all the more necessary because of the general ignorance in the midst of which we live. Earl Baldwin, a one-time Prime Minister, in one of his writings claimed that this is the most irreligious age the world has ever seen since Christ was born. Aldous Huxley said that this is an age of what he calls moral regression on a scale that has never been seen before. Dr Joad said in one of his books: 'For the first time in human history a generation has arisen that has no religion and that feels the need of none.' And if these writers belong to a previous generation, we cannot deceive ourselves that things are any better now.

If teaching is to be effective to any constituency like this, it must have certain features.

(a) It is only the best teachers who must be used. A distinguished university professor said the other day in my hearing that the best teachers in any university department should be allocated not to the advanced and honours classes, but to the first year and the backward and those whose knowledge was least adequate. If ever there was a need today, it is the need for the expert teacher. I cannot for the life of me see why there should be employed specialists in physical education and not in religious education. The situation is far too serious to leave to anything but the best.

(b) Clearly in such a situation teaching must be above all intelligible. If I were to give one single bit of advice to any preacher or teacher today, it would be: Never say anything to which you cannot attach a distinct and definite meaning. Nothing does more harm than the use of religious conventional jargon which is quite unintelligible to the outsider and which, if we were honest, means very little to ourselves.

(c) Clearly any teaching we attempt must be both interesting and relevant; and to do that it must start from the here

and now to get to the there and then. Any good lesson ought
to be summable in one single sentence. At the end of any
lesson it should be possible to ask: 'Now what was all that
about?', and to put the answer in one sentence.

(d) There is a sense—and to this I will return—in which
all good teaching must be individually aimed. There are
two ways of shooting: one with a shot gun which sprays off a
collection of pellets in the general direction of the object
desired to be hit; one with a rifle which fires a bullet direct
at one particular target. It is always a wrong thing to fire off
a lesson or sermon in the general direction of the audience.
We ought to take one or two people in the audience and talk
to—not at—them, preferably people whom we know to be
slow in the uptake. Everything should be tested by their
reaction. Brahms's advice to a young musician was: 'If you
are singing the most hackneyed song in the world, pick out
one man in the back row of the audience and sing it to him as
if he had never heard it in his life before.' Teaching cannot
be too direct.

(iii) Something to feel, something to remember, and lastly
we have to give those young people *something to do*. I think
that every lesson we teach should involve action, and that
before the next lesson is taught there should be a discussion
about how successful that action has been in the previous
week. The great danger with youth is to present religion as
if it were a series of questions to be answered and problems
to be solved rather than things to be done. It may well be
that our duty is to help people to express their religion just
as much as to help them to find it.

Lastly, and very briefly I want to summarize the ways in
which teaching can actually be done. There are four ways.

(i) There is the *lecture method*. Unquestionably it has its
place. There is a certain amount of factual information to
be transmitted and this is often the best way to do it. It is
especially valuable if it can be backed up with some reading,

and the cheap paperback makes that possible nowadays.

(ii) There is the *group discussion method*. But in this certain things must be remembered.

Too much group discussion is a pooling of ignorance. Group discussion comes best after information has been given. Secondly, the leader must be an expert. He must know at least some of the answers and must be at least a step ahead. Thirdly, every discussion should end in the statement of one certainty and must not evaporate in a series of unanswered questions. It must never become argument simply for argument's sake. Mental gymnastics are valuable, but not as an end in themselves.

(iii) There is *the project method*, learning by doing. It is excellent for a small group to learn by doing, to take some specifically Christian undertaking and to do it together.

(iv) I cannot help feeling that the last way is the most important of all; and that last way is simply *intimate private talk*. Not every person can listen to a lecture; in a discussion group the shy person is silent and the slick, confident talker monopolizes the conversation, and often the eccentric and the crank talk their heads off to the complete ruin of the whole discussion. The really good teacher will put himself into such a relationship with his young people that they will come to him and talk to him about anything. He will sit down and talk, not forcing religion into the conversation but letting it go where it leads. He will never be in a hurry; it will be fatal to look at his watch. Dr Johnson's great complaint about John Wesley was that Wesley was so busy that he never had time to cross his legs and have his talk out. I have not the slightest doubt that the best teaching will be done in the cafeteria and the lounge where we simply get to know each other and to talk.

And that leads to the final and all-important truth. All teaching depends on personal relationships. We have to begin by being the friends of those we teach.

6

Preaching in the Twentieth Century

IT is characteristic of all of us that we tend to think that the situation in which we personally are involved is the most difficult situation that has ever been and that ever can be. But there is a very real sense in which the human situation does not change. As the French proverb has it: 'The more things change the more they remain the same.' The voice of the *laudator temporis acti* has never been silent in the land, and there have never been wanting those who nostalgically sing the praises of the 'good old days'; but it is equally true that no one has ever taken out a new patent for the human heart. The basic ingredients of the human situation are precisely the same. Now one, now another may predominate; in one generation there may be one emphasis and in another another; but the basic essentials do not vary. Here is a quotation:

The world is passing through troublous times. The young people of today think of nothing but themselves. They have no reverence for parents or old age. They are impatient of all restraint. They talk as if they knew everything, and what passes for wisdom with us is foolishness with them. As for the girls, they are forward and immodest and unwomanly in speech, behaviour and dress.

That is clearly a quotation from a sermon; and the sermon was preached by Peter the Hermit in the year AD 1274. One would have thought that the days of the Reformation would

be one of the most thrilling times in the religious history of
the world, but even then Luther could write: 'This is the
devil's own age; gladly would I see myself and my people
snatched from it.' They say that one of the earliest scraps of
papyrus ever found, dating to about 2000 BC has only one
decipherable sentence on it: 'Things are not what they used
to be.' And as someone has said, when Adam and Eve left
the Garden of Eden, Adam may well have turned to Eve
and said: 'My dear, we are living in an age of transition.'
All this is so, and yet it is still true to say that every age has
certain identifiable characteristics; each age has its own
atmosphere. And there are certain characteristics of the
middle of the twentieth century which the preacher must
remember, if he is to speak to the condition of his people.

(i) First and foremost, we are living in *an age of fear*. There
can have been few ages which have looked forward with such
dread as our own generation looks to the future. C. E. M.
Joad once remarked that men have acquired the powers of
gods and that they use them like irresponsible schoolboys.
If that was true when Joad spoke it is still truer today. We
live in an age when men have acquired powers which may
well disintegrate the world and leave the earth a blasted
waste and a poison-infected desert. There are weapons today
which would not only devastate the world, but which would
also ruin the life and the bodies of generations yet unborn.

Even in between the two wars there were voices of fear and
pessimism. During that period Sir Philip Gibbs wrote his
Autobiography. The First World War was then past, the
second was still to come. He wrote:

If I smell poison-gas in Edgware Road I am not going to put on a
gas-mask or go to a gas-proof room. I am going out to take a
good sniff of it; for I shall know that the game is up.

We are living in a generation today which consciously or
unconsciously has the feeling that the game is up. 'Man',

This is God in history making
men aware of failure & need

said H. G. Wells—and again he was speaking before the situation had reached its present stage—'who began in a cave behind a windbreak will end in the disease-soaked ruins of a slum.' The climate is the climate of fear.

(ii) We may put this in another way which is equally true —we are living in an *age of pessimism*. The Victorian era was one of the most optimistic ages in history. It had a doctrine of a kind of effortless and automatic progress. Progress, so they thought, was like a river, flowing steadily onwards, and all that man had to do was to sit in his boat in the stream of this river of progress, and even without rowing he would be borne onwards and onwards to an ever-increasing perfection.

Inevitable
Progress

Along with this belief in progress went an almost astonishing faith in the power of education. Give us universal education, they seemed to say, and we shall educate not only the ignorance but also the sin out of men. 'Whatever be the perils in front of us,' said Lord Balfour in the nineteenth century, 'there are, so far, no symptoms at all either of pause or retrogression in the onward movement which for more than a thousand years has been characteristic of western civilization.'

Two world wars within the life-time of one man killed for ever the belief in automatic progress, and the plain fact that man's intellectual progress has far outstripped his moral progress has made it quite clear that, while a devil is bad, a clever devil is still worse. We live in an age which sees men, not steadily advancing towards a golden age of perfection, but rather suicidally drifting to chaos.

(iii) We live in *an age of uncertainty*, an age which has lost its faith. H. G. Wells contrasted the settled certainties of the Victorian age with the uncertainties of the time which followed:

Queen Victoria was like a great paper-weight who had sat on men's minds for fifty years, and when she was removed their ideas began to blow about haphazardly all over the place.

G

One of the first books which Mr Beverley Nichols wrote was entitled *Are they the same at Home?* and consisted of a series of interviews with certain famous people of his generation. One of the people he interviewed was Hilaire Belloc, one of the foremost Roman Catholics of his day. After his interview with Mr Belloc, Mr Nichols wrote: 'I was sorry for Mr Belloc, because I felt that he had nailed at least some of his colours to the wrong mast; but I was still sorrier for myself and my own generation, because I knew that we had no colours to nail to any mast.'

Jack Clemo, the poet, who in spite of blindness and deafness succeeded in somehow keeping his own faith, wrote a poem entitled *Max Gate*[1] in which he writes of the agnostic pessimism of Thomas Hardy:

> *You laboured with the unwindowed word,*
> *Blindly submissive, greyly passionate.*

He speaks of

> *The ache which spurred*
> *The tired hand onward with its task;*
> *The smouldering thought which dared not ask*
> *For signs of love within the irony.*

And then he writes

> *But you drew*
> *Back to the negative release,*
> *The closed curtain and the folded doubt.*

No gospel there. It was said of Matthew Arnold that he was a 'melancholy preacher who had mislaid his gospel'. And that is true of so many of the writers and the thinkers of this age.

G. K. Chesterton put this in another way. He said that there was a time when men saw things in terms of black and white, but that now they tended to see everything in terms of an indeterminate grey. Now there is a world of difference

[1] From *Map of Clay* (Methuen, 1961).

between this and the biblical point of view. E. F. F. Bishop has pointed out that in the semitic languages there is no word for *compromise*, because the idea does not exist, and that in the thought of the semitic peoples grey is not a colour. This is precisely one of the supreme difficulties of preaching today. If a man believes intensely in something, it is at least possible that he may be persuaded to believe equally intensely in something else; but if a man has lost the habit of belief altogether, if his slogan is, 'I couldn't care less', then the task of the preacher becomes desperately difficult. We live in a generation in which certainty is out of fashion and in which the intense conviction of faith has ceased in many people to exist.

(iv) In regard to the knowledge of the Bible this is *an age of ignorance*. There are very few circles now in which a knowledge of the Bible can be presupposed. W. E. Sangster in *Power in Preaching* quotes certain facts from a speech made by Admiral Sir Geoffrey Layton at Portsmouth. Lads who enter the Navy may be regarded as a fair cross-section of youth, and as somewhat above the average. On their entry to the Navy Sir Geoffrey set them a simple examination in Bible knowledge. As a result it was discovered that only 23 per cent could repeat the Lord's Prayer accurately; 28 per cent knew it in part; 49 per cent knew only the opening words. 72 per cent knew who Jesus Christ was, but only 39 per cent knew where he was born. 65 per cent knew what happened on Good Friday, but only 45 per cent knew about what happened at Easter, and fewer than 2 per cent knew what happened at Whitsun time.

One of the mysteries of the modern situation is the apparently complete ineffectiveness of religious education both in Church and in day-school. Quite certainly, even in the Church, the preacher cannot assume a familiarity with the biblical stories, and unexplained allusions to Scripture will seldom be understood.

(v) We live in an age where for many people the Church has become completely irrelevant. Dr Joad said in one of his books: 'For the first time in human history a generation has arisen that has no religion and that feels the need of none.' To a generation like that it is clear that the Church must stand for absolutely nothing.

(vi) There is one further factor in the situation which ought to be noticed. It was a commonplace in previous generations up to very recent times that, even if people had no use for Christian theology and Christian doctrine, they still unquestioningly accepted the Christian ethic. It was in fact quite common to say, 'Let us scrap Christian theology and let us concentrate on the ethical teaching of Jesus, about which everyone agrees.' Aldous Huxley has said that this is an age of moral regression on a scale that has never been known before. The new factor is that for the first time in history there is a widespread denial not only of Christian theology but also of the Christian ethic.

There are today crimes of robbery and violence on an unprecedented scale. There is a laxity in the relationship between the sexes such as has not been since Christianity came into the world as a force and a dynamic. The figures for divorce and for illegitimacy are terrifyingly large. There is a very large number of people who simply do not accept the Christian attitude to sex any longer. In past generations, even if people broke the Christian ethic, they none the less did not really question its rightness. But now they do. What are we to say of a society which has to organize special school classes for schoolgirls who are unmarried mothers? At this present time it is not simply the Church and its doctrine which are in danger. The whole conception of a Christian ethic and a Christian society is under attack. It is no small addition to the difficulties of the task of the preacher that he can no longer be certain that the people he desires to win accept the Christian ethic. He can no longer assume that it is enough to exhort them to obey and to live by that which they know is right; he has now in many cases to convince them that it is right.

So far we have been thinking of the world in which the task of the Church and the task of preaching lies. But let us turn our eyes and our thoughts nearer home; let us think of the Church itself. The Church will always have its saints and its prophets and the Church has its saints and its prophets today; but no one could really hold that this is one of the great ages of the Church. If one travels a great deal about the country by road, one comes to a grim conclusion about the Church. Simply by looking at the Church's buildings, at the externals of the Church, one would undoubtedly reach the conclusion that in this country the Church once *was* a great institution but that now it has fallen on evil days and that it is in decay. All over the country you will see derelict churches, churches in ruins and churches used for other purposes; all over the country you will see churches in disrepair, shabby, dingy, unkempt, their grounds a wilderness, their doors unpainted, their grass uncut, their windows cracked or lacking panes of glass. There is little enough excuse for this, for much could be done by voluntary labour; but it may be that even that is now impossible, for I heard recently of a small country charge in which only two of the members were not old-age pensioners. That these things should be so is a tragedy and it is the worst kind of propaganda that anyone could imagine; the image of the Church is so often the image of someone who has fallen on evil days, the image of an institution with a noble past, a struggling present, and no future. No one could say that this is one of the ages when the Church surges and pulsates with vitality, and when the Church stands as a dynamic and dominant figure in the life of the nation. And there are certain reasons for this. The faults are not all on the world's side; there are faults within the Church as well.

(i) In too many of the Church's members there tends to be *interest without commitment*. There is a very great deal of interest in religion today. A flood of theological books flows from the printing presses, and many of them become best-sellers in their own right. Even the great Sunday newspapers will give their centre pages to the latest developments in the technique of New Testament critical methods. It is not diffi-cult today to organize discussion groups on Christian ques-tions and problems.

But there is all the difference in the world between enlist-ing in an Army and joining a club. If a man enlists in the Army, he accepts an obedience and a discipline which are absolute; he submits his will to a higher authority; he abandons the right to run his own life and to make his own decisions. On the other hand, when a man joins a club he can go to it when he likes and he can stay away when he likes; he can give it as much or as little of his life and his time as he likes; he can play as much or as little a part in its activities as he wishes. He has no really binding obligation to it. There are too many Christians for whom membership of the Church is far more like joining a club than it is like enlisting in an Army.

If we are interested in Jesus Christ it means that He is one of the competing interests in life; if we are committed to Him it means that He is the dominant dynamic of life—and noth-ing else will really do.

(ii) There is in the Church today—as in fact there has always been—a tendency *to substitute things which are good enough in themselves but which are none the less not central for the things which really lie at the centre of the Christian faith*. It is not that the things which are used as substitutes are bad things; it is that they are secondary things. They are the kind of things which are excellent means, but which are out of proportion when they become ends. And it is usually the case that the substitution is quite unconscious, and those who make it are unaware that they are evading the real issues. Of these substitutions there are two which may specially be mentioned.

(*a*) There is the substitution of theological discussion for real devotion. We have seen very recently how a book like *Honest to God* can have a sale that would make a popular novelist envious, how it can be discussed, talked and argued about, welcomed, repudiated, regarded as the utterance of a prophet or denounced as the propaganda of the devil, how it can come to occupy the centre pages and the correspondence columns of the great newspapers, but, when all is said and done, it is very doubtful if it made any difference to the religious life of the nation.

J. S. Whale once said that the trouble so often is that we sit round the fire with a pipe in the mouth and the feet on the mantelpiece and discuss theories of the Atonement instead of bowing down before the wounds of Christ. We are far from saying that such discussion is not necessary; it is essential; but it is not an end in itself; and there can be in a Church or in a College a ferment of exciting theological discussion while at the same time real fellowship and real devotion have evaporated away.

(*b*) There has always been a tendency in some Churches and in some congregations to substitute ritual elaboration and liturgical perfection for true religion. Again, let no one think that these things are to be despised and underrated. They are not to be neglected. But quite recently I heard a parson say that his one desire before he left his parish was to introduce Gregorian chanting. It is possible to love a liturgy more than you love people; it is possible to be more concerned with the way in which the thing is done than with the number of people who are there to share in it.

The basic fact is that intense theological discussion and devotion to liturgical perfection are much less costly than real religion which is love of God expressed in love of man.

It is so tragically possible for the Church to withdraw within the ivory tower of theology and liturgy and to forget that the men for whom Christ died are in the market-place and on the streets.

(iii) This leads us to the third danger in the present-day Church. It may well be true that the Church today in this country has lost its missionary dynamic, and by the word *missionary* I am not thinking of work overseas but of work within this country. In Colossians 1[28] Paul proclaims his one object: 'Him we proclaim, warning *every man*, and teaching *every man* in all wisdom, that we may present *every man* mature in Christ.' Surely we cannot help noticing the thrice repeated *every man*. The passion of Paul was to gather every man into the love of God. Myers in his poem *Saint Paul* finely made Paul say:

> *Only I see like souls the folk thereunder,*
> *Bound who should conquer, slaves who should be kings,*
> *Hearing their one hope with an empty wonder,*
> *Sadly contented with a show of things.*
>
> *Then with a thrill the intolerable craving*
> *Shivers throughout me like a trumpet call,*
> *O to save these, to perish for their saving,*
> *Die for their life, be offered for them all!*

Is this spirit still within the modern Church? Is it not true that the Church of today in this country has become a respectable middle-class institution which has largely lost both the top and the bottom ends of the social scale? And I think that it may well be that there is more than one of us who could point to cases where, when an attempt was made to contact and bring in those who are hostile to the Church and who are social problems, that attempt was looked on askance and was even forcibly terminated because the middle-class respectability of some congregation was shocked and disturbed with contact with a level of society which it did not know and which it did not want to know. The real gravamen of this situation is not so much that the Church is so often a middle-class institution but that it is content to be so and to remain so.

It is within this situation and against this background that our preaching is to be done. What then shall it be like? Dr C. H. Dodd distinguished three kinds of preaching within the early Church. There was KĒRUGMA. *Kērugma* means a herald's pronouncement, and *kērugma* is the plain statement of the facts of the Christian faith and the contents of Christian belief. *Kērugma* does not so much argue and defend and justify as it does proclaim the Christian message. It says: 'This is what I believe.' There is DIDACHĒ. *Didachē* means teaching and *didachē* is the explanation and the application of the Christian message. In *didaché* there is a strong ethical element, for it tells the Christian how a redeemed and forgiven man ought to live. The Sermon on the Mount is the perfect example of *didaché*. But obviously *didachē* must be preceded by *kérugma*, for *didachē* draws out and systematizes the implications of *kērugma*. It instructs a man in the Christian faith and in the Christian life. There is PARAKLĒSIS. *Paraklēsis* means exhortation, and *paraklēsis* exhorts, pleads with, and urges a man to accept the Christian faith and to live the Christian life. Clearly *paraklésis* must be preceded by both *kērugma* and *didachē*, for there is no point in exhorting a man to accept a faith the content of which he has never been instructed. Lastly there is HOMILIA. *Homilia* is the general discussion of any subject in the light of the Christian faith and the Christian Gospel. And *homilia* can obviously only effectively come when the hearer has already been taught and instructed in the substance and the content and the implications of the Christian faith.

When we set the modern situation beside this, we are bound to see how far out of proportion modern preaching has become. In modern preaching there is not very much *kērugma*. I am quite certain, for instance, that we should preach our way through the Apostles' Creed and the great doctrines of the faith at least once in every three years. But how often is this done ? When, for instance, did you last hear a sermon on justification by faith, which is the very foundation pillar of the reformed faith ? When did you last hear a sermon on sanctification, which is the very essence of the Christian life ? There is tragically little *didachē*. The biggest single fault with the pulpit in these modern days is that it has so largely neglected the teaching ministry. And yet how much easier for the preacher as well as how much more beneficial for the congregation the teaching ministry is. If a man is systematically expounding the Christian faith he will never lack for material, and he will never be desperately casting about on a Saturday evening for something to preach about on the Sunday. There is a vast amount of *paraklēsis*, of exhortation, but, as we have already implied, what use is there in exhorting a man to accept and to live a faith which he does not understand ? There is an extraordinary amount of *homilia*, the general treatment of any subject under the broad light of the Christian religion. And here again is the disaster. One of the biggest mistakes of the modern pulpit is the substitution of the topical for the biblical sermon. It may be unfair to say so, and it may be going too far to say so, and in many cases it will be untrue to say so, but there are far too many preachers who take their topics far more from the daily newspapers than they do from the Bible. And the plain fact is that people do not come to Church to hear a preacher's opinions about this or that topical question. Certainly that will amuse and interest a certain number of people, but people come to Church because they are bewildered with life's problems, and they are beset by life's temptations, and they are wounded by life's sorrows, and they are tired with life's exhaustion, and they want some word from the Lord. This is far from saying that the preacher will never mention the burning questions of the day, but it is to say that they will emerge from his exposition of the word of the Lord and will not dominate it.

The exposition of Scripture, the proclamation of the faith, the teaching of the Christian way must be the dominant notes of preaching

What then must this preaching be like?

(i) To begin with the very first essential, *it must be intelligible.* There is still an enormous amount of theological jargon talked in pulpits and in religious books. Sangster in one of his books on preaching quotes from a mission report which at that time was actually on his desk:

We meditate on our heavenly Father's past mercies. Hitherto hath the Lord helped us, and, for the present, Jehovah Jireh. We earnestly look for his coming again, when he shall see of the travail of his soul and be satisfied, and, whatever the future, here or hereafter, it is 'Hallelujah'. Should he in his long-suffering tarry, then we know that this also is well, and that he will always honour our faith and dependence and obedience to his word.

Sangster's reaction was that, if this was sent out as an appeal to any ordinary business man, it might as well be written in a foreign language. Sangster goes on to quote the result of the investigations of a certain Dr William D. White. Dr White made a personal investigation into preacher's words and phrases which his people did not understand. The list included the following—dayspring, logos, husbandman, washed in the blood, blood of the lamb, cherubim, seraphim, throne of mercy, heir of salvation, alpha and omega, things of the flesh, balm in Gilead, the bosom of Abraham, in Christ, and many another.

We ought to remember the example of John Wesley, who was an Oxford don. In so far as Wesley was proud of anything he was proud of the fact that he was a fellow of Lincoln College; and yet this Wesley could hold spellbound the miners at the pithead or the crowd on Kennington Common.

In his early days he had a custom: he would take the manu-script of his sermon and read it to a simple, uneducated, old domestic servant, and he would urge her to stop him every time he said something which she did not understand. The manuscript became a mass of erasures and interlinings, but Wesley developed a speaking style that was so clear that the simplest person could understand. Writing in 1746 Wesley said:

I design plain truth for plain people; therefore, of set purpose I abstain from all nice and philosophical speculations; from all perplexed and intimate reasonings; and, as far as possible, from even the show of learning. I labour to avoid all words which are not easy to understand, all which are not used in common life; and, in particular, those kinds of technical terms that so fre-quently occur in Bodies of Divinity; those modes of speaking which men of reading are intimately acquainted with, but which to the common people are an unknown tongue.

In giving advice on this matter Wesley writes:

Clearness in particular is necessary for you and for me, because we are to instruct people of the lowest understanding. Therefore we above all, if we think with the wise, yet must speak with the vulgar. We should constantly use the most common, little, easy words (so they are pure and proper) which our language affords.

James Black tells somewhere how he went to Alexander Whyte when he was asked to come to the then famous pulpit of Broughton Place Church in Edinburgh for advice as to whether or not he should accept the call. Whyte asked one question. 'Can you clarify your thought?' he asked. Black answered that he was fairly certain that he could clarify whatever thought he had. 'If you can clarify your thought,' said Whyte, 'you can go anywhere.' W. M. Macgregor said of A. B. Bruce: 'He did not cloudily guess at things; he saw them.' Sangster liked the inspired misquotation: 'Though I speak with the tongues of men and angels and have not *clarity*, I am become as sounding brass and a tinkling cymbal.'

There is an idea which dies hard but which deserves to be finally disposed of and for ever interred. It is often said that, just as every other science has a technical vocabulary, so has religion; and that just as a man will learn the technical vocabulary of, say, electricity and will speak of volts and amperes and kilowatts, and direct and alternating current and so on, so he must learn the technical vocabulary of religion. There is a towering fallacy in that analogy. There is no science which is every man's life business. A man can go comfortably through life knowing not the first technical thing about electricity; it will certainly not affect his eternal destiny if he does not know how electricity works. But if theology is anything it is every man's business; it affects the soul of every man; for every man it is a matter of life and death; and therefore it must be intelligible to every man. A theology which cannot be communicated has something badly wrong with it. As Vincent Taylor once said: 'The test of a good theologian is—Can he write a tract?' A technical and esoteric vocabulary may be a necessity for some sciences; it can never be a necessity for a living theology.

There is an even wider way in which to express all this. *Religion, if it is true religion, must always be contemporary.* Here, I am convinced, is one of the great errors of the Church. There is about so much religion a quality of archaism. We worship in buildings which are Gothic or pseudo-Gothic; we express our belief in a Creed that is some eighteen hundred years old and that is expressed in terms of Greek philosophy; we commonly read the Scripture and often pray in a language that no one has used for something like three hundred years; a parson will appear clothed in robes which are relics of the robes of the medieval monks and friars. The whole atmosphere is something which belongs to the past. Now there is one simple historical fact which shows how wrong we are; if the New Testament was not unique as the fundamental document of the Christian faith, it would still be linguistically unique as the sole literary surviving document containing the contemporary colloquial Greek of its day. The New Testament is written in the Greek of the common people. Nothing could possibly be more unfitting than to read it in Elizabethan English. If it is to sound as it sounded to those who first read it, it ought to be in the language of the common people and of everyday, not in slang, but in straightforward ordinary language. We are similarly in error with the language of prayer. There can be no good reason why the language of prayer was stereotyped and fossilized in the sixteenth-century English of Cranmer and Laud.

Will you remember one fact? The name by which Jesus called God, and in the name by which we are taught to call him, is Abba, Father. Now Abba is the name by which a young child called his father in the home circle in Palestine, as he still does today. If you found it in any ordinary document there is only one translation of it—Daddy. Now I am not saying that we should call God that, but I am pleading that we should be done for ever with thou's and thee's and vouchsafe's and beseech's; and that we should use in preaching, in scripture and in worship the best and the simplest language of our own day and generation. It may be that we who have been born and bred in the Church love the old cadences, but are we going to be selfish enough to demand what we sentimentally like while there are millions outside to whom religion will never become a living reality until it talks to them in the language of the common people?

We will certainly not even begin to get anywhere unless we are intelligible and we shall not begin to be intelligible until we are contemporary.

(ii) Our preaching must not only be intelligible, *it must also be intelligent.* J. S. Whale has said: 'It is a moral duty to be intelligent.' And E. F. Scott has said that more often than we realize the failure of Christianity as a moral power is due to nothing other than intellectual sloth.

If there is one thing that a sermon needs to be it is that it needs to be prepared. David refused to render to God that which cost him nothing—and that is precisely what so many preachers offer Him. When you approach the Bible you should approach it with every help and every aid that scholarship has given us. It has been said that in law ignorance may be a possible defence, but neglect of knowledge never is. I can think of no greater arrogance of mind than for a man to approach a passage of Scripture and to seek to preach upon it without at least trying to find out what the saints and the scholars of the past and the present have said about it. Surely no man thinks that his puny mind can say the last word about any passage of Scripture.

Every sermon should be written out word by word—and there is no exception to that rule. If a man will not accept the discipline of setting down his thoughts on paper in an orderly and careful way he should not take upon himself the privilege of preaching. It may be that some will say, 'What place does this leave for the Holy Spirit?' There is a kind of person and preacher who claims to be entirely dependent on the Holy Spirit. F. C. Grant tells how a meeting was given some instruction in the methods of Bible-study. At the end of it a girl rose and said that the whole thing was needless. 'All you need to do,' she said, 'is to open the Bible, take any six verses, and the Holy Spirit will do the rest.' The best commentary on that is from W. E. Sangster's valuable book, *Power in Preaching.* Sangster writes:

The Rev. Greville Lewis was once conducting a conference of lay preachers. He had made a moving plea for the consecration of the whole mind to the service of the pulpit, but when the conference was thrown open for discussion one lay preacher present rejected both the argument and the appeal. Study and thought and sermon outlines, he said, were all unnecessary. At least they were unnecessary for *him*. He just prayed. Just that. Having prayed he went to his appointment, opened the Bible for the text, and the Holy Spirit did the rest. He concluded by saying: 'I have never failed for a message yet.'

The uncomfortable silence which followed this flat contradiction of everything the lecturer said was finally broken by a man who appeared to be profane. 'I never knew the Holy Spirit was so boring, repetitive and unoriginal,' he said. Urged to explain himself, he told the company that he worshipped at a church to which the previous speaker regularly came to preach. 'I've heard him many, many times,' he said. 'The only thing that varies in what he says is the text. He certainly opens the Bible and takes a phrase at random, but, whatever the text, after the first couple of sentences he always preaches the same uninspiring sermon. If he ever failed to appear, we could say it for him. You will notice how difficult I find it to accept his own explanation of his preaching. It would compel me to believe the impossible—that the Third Person of the Trinity had nothing fresh, and nothing moving and nothing mighty to say.'

R. C. Gillie once said: 'Prepare as if there was no such person as the Holy Spirit; preach as if there was no one but the Holy Spirit.' Believe me, the Spirit is even more operative when a man studies over his books, companies with the great saints and thinkers and writers of devotion. The greatest help of the Spirit comes to him who uses to the utmost the mind God gave him.

There is another aspect of this approach of the intelligence to the matters of religion. If we study the methods of Paul we find a very significant and suggestive fact. Beginning in Thessalonica and from then on consistently it is said of Paul that he *argued* with those who would talk with and listen to him. The word is *dialegesthai*, the word from which *dialectic* comes, and it is the very same word as is used to describe Socrates' method of question and answer in his teaching in Athens.

bulletins ask in topics the people want

There is something to be learned here. Here is the idea that preaching ought to be a dialogue as much as it is a monologue. Preaching has been too much one man telling other men, and too little a fellowship of believers and seekers thinking things over together. It may well be that we have been giving too little attention to the questions that the seekers and the believers wish to ask, and that we ought to use more and more a method in which teacher and taught, leader and seeker, seek the truth together. There can at least be no doubt that the appeal of preaching should be to the total personality, and that the mind is involved at least as much as the heart.

When we are thinking of the appeal of preaching to the mind and to the intelligence, it will be right to say here what has been said over and over again by implication—*it is essential that preaching should be systematic.* A man should preach to a scheme and plan whereby the whole Bible and the whole Christian faith are duly covered. It is fatal to leave the choice of subject to random last-minute choice. To preach to a scheme and plan will have far more than one advantage.

First, it will save the preacher from that last desperate evening-before search for a subject; he will know far ahead what he intends to preach about. Secondly, it will ensure that his congregation get a properly proportioned view of the Christian faith. Thirdly—and most important of all—it will save the congregation from being at the mercy of the preference and the whim of the preacher. Unless the preacher systematically plans, he will continue to preach on those things which mean most to him and those things which are in the forefront of his mind. When this happens you get unbalanced preaching. We know for instance the kind of preacher who preaches the second coming in season and out of season. We know the pacifist who cannot keep pacifism out of his sermons. We know the kind of preacher who does

H

nothing but thunder denunciation and the kind of preacher who does nothing but preach an almost sentimentalized love. To whom, we must add the preacher who is all *Honest to God*, or all religion and politics. If we preach only about the things we want to preach about, we will necessarily preach a sadly truncated gospel. There is nothing so good for the preacher as to prepare and preach a sermon on a book of the Bible which has never really attracted him, on a doctrine which he has never really thought about, on some question of the faith which he has hitherto evaded. If we are going to face the task of Christian education which is the essential duty of the pulpit and the preacher, then we have to see to it that we are dominated, not by our own preferences and prejudices, but by the realization of the obligation to preach the whole Gospel.

(iii) It may be said that up to this point we have been thinking about the connection of preaching with the mind. But there are other sides of the human personality to which we must now turn. *The preacher must challenge the will*. The preacher is not concerned only to produce people who have acquired a certain amount of knowledge. He is concerned to produce people who have also taken certain decisions, the decision to accept the offer of God in Jesus Christ and the decision to live a certain kind of life.

One of the oddest features of the present-day situation is that conversion is not connected with the Church. By and large, people do not expect conversion to happen in the Church; they look for it to happen at missions and campaigns and at types of service which are not usually connected with the Church at all. It is almost true to say that there is something very like a suspicion of conversion in the orthodox and conventional Church. It is certainly not true that preaching should always be evangelistically and emotionally demanding conversion; but it is true that preaching must always be preaching for a verdict. It must be either explicitly or implicitly saying to a man, 'Choose you this day whom you will serve.'

John Kennedy, in his recent book on preaching, quotes a story that the late Johnstone Jeffrey used often to tell. Once two friends, one of them a parson, found themselves in a fair-ground. One of the side-shows was a knife-throwing act. One of the partners was strapped to a board; the other flung knives at her; and the knives sank quivering into the board only inches from her body. The layman turned to the parson, and said: 'That's like your preaching, Fred. It never draws blood!'

Ultimately all preaching must be the attempt to reconcile men to God through Jesus Christ; and therefore the preacher must continuously confront the hearer with the challenge of the Gospel of Christ and the invitation to the pilgrimage of the Christian life. It is very significant that the New Testament never calls Christianity a system of thought; it never calls it a philosophy; it never, surprisingly enough, calls it a religion; it calls it THE WAY. Preaching must therefore be a challenge to the will to accept Jesus Christ, to witness to the fact that we have accepted Him, and to set out upon His way. It may well be that there ought to be in our preaching far more room for decision than there normally is.

(iv) So then preaching should equip and educate the mind; preaching should challenge and kindle the will. But there is still another part of man. *Preaching must speak to the heart.* No man will ever be a preacher unless he bears his people on his heart. The one thing that the preacher must never forget is the human need of the people before him.

It may be the basic mistake that so many of us preachers make is just that we forget the human condition of the people in front of us. I am not now a pastor, but in three consecutive days three telephone calls came to me. One was from a woman of my own age, an old school friend, a widow, whose only son, a brilliant young Regular Army officer, was killed in a quite inexplicable motor smash on the A1. The second was to give me news of one of my own students whose car, driven with all care, had skidded on a country road on his way home, and who was lying in hospital with a compound fracture of the leg and a broken neck, and he has a wife and four-month-old baby. The third was from a woman whose only daughter of twenty-one had been electrocuted in bed by an electric blanket, an event which was almost unbelievable, and which the courts, God forgive them, called an act of God. Just a year ago in my own College two of my students were in trouble. Of one the father died—a session clerk and a godly man—without warning, the day before he was to be licensed as a preacher. To the other, a young man who had been an army physical instructor and who has a lovely wife and three perfect children there was born a mongol child. This is what is happening.

'Never morning wore to evening but some heart did break.' Now suppose a man's heart is breaking and a mother's heart is wounded, suppose a man is wrestling with some temptation, suppose a man is haunted by the sense of his failure and his defeat, suppose a man is worried to death. Just on Sunday a woman told me of a stay that she had in hospital a short time ago. She was a walking-case and she went into the washroom. There was a girl there, twenty-three years old, who was sitting very quietly, almost like stone, looking at her own face in a mirror. My friend said to her: 'Are you all right?' 'I suppose so,' said the girl, 'but I have just received the sentence of death. I have a disease, they tell me, and if they don't find a cure in a year—and so far there is no cure—I will be dead. I'm an only child, and I don't know how to tell my parents.'

The world is full of this. Now suppose I am going through this, suppose even that you are like me and you are not actually going through it but the weight of someone's sorrow is on your heart, and then suppose you go to Church and you

get a tirade against *That was the Week That Was*, or you get
someone's half-baked opinions about the political situation,
or you get a violent denunciation of Roman Catholicism, or
something like that—what comfort is in that? There was
once a man who left a certain congregation, in which the
preacher had a notable talent for denunciation. He was
asked why he left. 'I was tired,' he said, 'at getting a handful
of gravel flung in my face every Sunday.'

You will remember Leslie J. Tizard, that brilliant young
preacher who was stricken with inoperable cancer. In the
last section of his book *Facing Life and Death* he tells us of his
feelings; he tells us how the shallowness of so much preaching suddenly dawned on him. Then he quotes a saying of
J. B. Priestley: 'People get a bit sick of having the front of
their minds tickled, when they want something that goes
deeper.'

God forgive the preacher who either in his sermon or in
his prayers does not bring the comfort and the grace of God
to those who need them. Long ago Epictetus said: 'Vain is
the discourse of philosophy by which no suffering is healed.'
Let no preacher ever forget that he is the bringer of the
comfort of God.

(v) There remains only one thing more to say. *The
preparation of the message is important, but the preparation
of the preacher is even more important.* No man can teach
what he does not know; and no man can create a love for
Jesus Christ that he does not feel. 'I preached', said John
Bunyan, 'what I felt, what I smartingly did feel.' L. P.
Jacks once said a thing that makes you think: 'Every preacher
should ask himself now and again how far he is preaching
what he really believes, and how far what he wants others to
believe.'

From the great preacher something radiates. Even when
you do not understand him you still feel the presence of the
divine. Thirty years ago and more now I was assistant to

Duncan Blair in Glasgow. He was a mystic; he could walk in realms which to the rest of us were shut; often, I think, the congregation did not know what was going on; but the people loved him, for they never came out of that Church without feeling that God had been there, and to this day they talk of him.

Any preacher to whom Christ is real will make Christ real to others. Above all we need this note of personal conviction. Tillotson the Archbishop of Canterbury and Betterton the famous actor were close friends. 'Why is it', Tillotson used to say to Betterton, 'that you on the stage can move people to tears, while I in the pulpit with the world-shaking message of Christianity leave them quite unmoved?' 'Because', said Betterton, 'you are telling them stories while I am showing them facts.' What a condemnation of preaching that the fancies of the stage had more reality than the blazing truths of Christianity! 'Your theologians', said Rhadhakrishnan the great Indian mystic, 'seem to me like men talking in their sleep.' Longinus the great Greek literary critic wrote the famous book *On the Sublime*. 'Sublimity', he said, 'is the echo of a great soul.' The word he used for *echo* is the Greek word for the ring of a coin which shows whether it is genuine or not. The man who knows Christ cannot keep the ring of it out of his voice and his preaching.

Quayle, the great American preacher, has a passage on preaching:

Preaching is the art of making a sermon and delivering it. Why no! Preaching is the art of making a preacher and delivering that. Preaching is the outrush of the soul in speech. Therefore the elemental business in preaching is not with the preaching but with the preacher. It is no trouble to preach but a vast trouble to construct a preacher. What then in the light of this is the task of a preacher? Mainly this, the amassing of a great soul so as to have something worth while to give—the sermon is the preacher up to date.

The sermon is the preacher.

Life is very full nowadays; the life of the Church and of every congregation is very variegated and complicated. We must get and keep the centre right. For sixteen years I had the privilege of serving that great scholar and saint and mystic G. H. C. Macgregor. I often heard him speak to students when they first came to College. He would tell them of all the work they had to do and then he would tell them of a saying of Richard Bentley the great eighteenth-century classicist. Bentley would tell young scholars and students that amid all the many minutiae of grammar and syntax and textual criticism they must never lose sight of the *res ipsa*, the thing itself. For the preacher there is only one thing which is the *thing itself*. Once a young artist came to Doré with a picture of Jesus that he had painted. He asked Doré for his criticism. Doré was silent. The young man pressed him, and quietly Doré answered: 'You don't love him or you would paint him better.' In the last analysis our preaching depends on nothing other than our love of Jesus Christ and our love for the men for whom Christ died.

7

The Word through Books

SUPERLATIVES are always dangerous, but it is certainly true
to say that this is more than any other previous age the age
of the book. Books today have a place in the life of society
and in the life of the community such as they never had
before. There are three quite general reasons for that. There
is the mass production of books, which can be at a speed
and in a number never before really possible. There is
the price of the book. Even the most authoritative and the
most technical of books can now become paper-backs to be
bought at a few shillings. There is the wide dissemination of
the book. No longer is the book confined to the booksellers,
but you will find it in the tobacconist's, the confectioner's,
even the grocer's, on the railway station and the air-terminal
counter, and now the book has even reached the slot-machine
in places like hotels and the pavement's edge on the streets of
the great cities.

This has had one notable effect. It has created a new
reading-public. Even forty years ago a very large section of
the public would not have thought of going into a bookshop;
that was the preserve of the academic, the cultured and the
leisured world; but now it is often the case that the reader
graduates from the shop at the corner to the bookshop
proper, for the paper-backs now available to him at the little
shop will take him far beyond the world of fiction into the
realm of philosophy and science and theology. It might seem
natural for the bookseller proper to resent the bookselling

of the tobacconist or the confectioner, but it is precisely from those who started buying books there that in the end he will draw his best and his most discerning customers in the future.

It is difficult for us in the mid-twentieth century to realize just what a revolution this is. For that reason it is worth while to take a quick glance at the history of the book.

(i) The earliest substance on which books were written was papyrus. Papyrus was made from the pith of a certain kind of bulrush, as thick as a man's arm, which grows only on the banks of the Nile. The papyrus was cut with a sharp knife into very thin strips; the strips were laid first horizontally and then vertically; they were moistened with Nile water and glue and then subjected to pressure; they were then smoothed off with pumice stone. The resulting substance was rather like brown paper. So long as damp does not get at it, it is practically indestructible. The oldest papyrus fragment dates from 3600 BC and is a sheet of accounts from the reign of the Egyptian king Assa.

Papyrus was manufactured in sheets measuring ten by eight inches. And here is the first notable fact—the cheapest papyrus cost fourpence a sheet and the most expensive one shilling and twopence. At this stage the book had not yet emerged in its present form. The sheets were laid and joined edge to edge horizontally in one long strip and then rolled up, and the book was in fact a roll, and remained such until at least the beginning of the Christian era. The roll, often fixed to a wooden roller at each end, was unrolled with one hand, as it was read, and rolled up with the other. The maximum length of a papyrus roll for all practical purposes was thirty feet, which is almost exactly the length of roll needed to hold Matthew's or Luke's Gospel. This meant that a book could never be long. The writing was in narrow upright columns right across the strip; and it meant, as we can easily calculate, that the cheapest papyrus would cost at least ten shillings for a thirty-foot roll.

At this stage it is quite clear that books must have been the perquisite of the few. They were well known and quite common. In the fifth century BC Socrates can say that you can buy the writings of Anaxagoras anywhere, and that books contain the treasures which the wise have left. In the great library of Alexandria there were 700,000 rolls and in the library of Pergamum 200,000. Books were well known, but they were not yet within the price-range of things that the ordinary person, apart from the wealthy and the scholar, would be able to possess.

(ii) The second great stage in the history of the book came with the introduction of vellum as the material on which to write. Vellum is technically the skin of calves, but the skins of other animals were also used. The very best and the very finest vellum was made of the skins of still unborn calves, taken before their birth from their mother's womb. With the coming of vellum there came also the book in its modern form. As we have seen, in the time of the use of papyrus the book was in the form of the roll. That was partly at least due to the fact that papyrus can be rolled, but not folded. It is brittle, and if it is folded it will crack. But vellum could be folded and folded and folded again to make the quires of material out of which a book is made. So then the book now assumes its present form.

By Roman times, by the time of Cicero, the bookshop was a popular place of meeting in Rome. There were advertisements on its pillars; the shops became popular meeting-places and literary salons, features of educated and cultured Rome.

We are now coming to the first faint beginnings of mass production. Of course, at this time books were still all hand-written. A book could be mass-produced by being dictated to a room full of scribes. This had the obvious disadvantage that any book so dictated would quite certainly be full of misspellings and mistakes. We actually have some information about the speed of production. There are fourteen books of Martial's epigrams. In the Loeb classical library edition the Latin text of the epigrams takes up about 500 small pages of print. A copy dictated took about seventeen hours to write, and it was possible to produce an edition of 1,000 in a month. So in the ancient world a rate of 1,000 copies a month was a high rate of production. In the first book of the epigrams there are about 700 lines of poetry and, mass-produced and properly bound, it sold for 5 denarii, that is, for a little less than five shillings, which is a high price for an inevitably not very accurate copy of 500 lines of poetry.

For proper, professional, good copying we have the actual scale of charges. The contents of a book in the ancient world were reckoned in terms of *stichoi*. A *stichos* is not a line; a book was not counted in lines, because different editions would have different numbers of lines according to the size of the paper and of the script. It was reckoned in *stichoi*. A *stichoi* was defined as the average length of a Homeric hexameter line, which is sixteen syllables. So a book was reckoned in terms of the number of units of that length which it contained. There is one New Testament manuscript, the *Codex Claromontanus*, which has a list of the number of *stichoi* in every New Testament book. The number of *stichoi*, for instance, in Matthew is 2,500. The number of *stichoi* in the four Gospels plus Acts is 11,400; and the number of *stichoi* in the whole New Testament is 18,302. Now in AD 301 there was issued an edict of Diocletian which fixed practically all prices; it is a very early example of governmental price-fixing. One of the things that were fixed was the pay of a scribe, and the pay of a professional scribe was from twenty to twenty-five denarii per hundred *stichoi*, which is practically one pound per hundred *stichoi*. So then we see that to buy a properly scribed copy of the four Gospels plus Acts would cost £114, and a copy of the whole New Testament would cost not far short of £200.

The contrast with the modern situation is immense. It is quite clear that very few people, and even very few institutions, could possess a properly scribed and produced book. The cost of the whole Bible including both the Old and the New Testaments would be not very far short of £1,000. The contrast between that and, say, the Fontana edition of the *Revised Standard Version* is staggering.

(iii) The third stage was in the tenth century when paper first arrived from the east; and when in the fifteenth century printing came upon the scene the way of the cheap and mass-produced book was wide open.

It was by no means everyone who approved of the development of the book. Some people, including Socrates, looked on the book as a disaster. There were two main objections to the book.

(i) The arrival of the book, even in the limited form in which it existed in papyrus rolls in the fifth and fourth century BC, was regarded by many as involving the necessary death of the memory. An Egyptian king called books the elixirs of memory, but many held—and perhaps rightly—that the opposite was the case. Before the books emerged, there was only one way of possessing that which had been said, and that was to store it in the memory. Xenophon tells of the excellent and cultured Greek gentleman Niceratus, and Niceratus told how his father, wishing him to grow up a good man, made him learn by heart the whole *Iliad* and the whole *Odyssey*. There are twenty-four books, each averaging about 700 lines, in each of them. That is to say that Niceratus —and he was only typical of his contemporaries—knew by heart forty-eight times 700 lines of poetry. T. R. Glover tells how in Finland right down to modern times—perhaps even yet—the young people learned the *Kalevala*, the national epic, by heart.

Now the book makes this quite unnecessary. It is quite true that there have been modern instances—for example, when people were prisoners in solitary confinement and in concentration camps with everything taken from them—when men thanked God for the passages of the Bible and the verses of hymns which they had stored in their minds, as Hans Lilje tells. But any wise teacher and any wise student will know that it is a first rule of study never to burden your mind with that which can be readily and easily found. Scholarship, as was pointed out far back in classical times, consists not so much in knowing things as in knowing where to find them when we want them. Therefore, it is a first rule of study never to clutter the memory with that which can be found at any moment. For instance, there can be few greater wastages of time and effort than learning the order of the books of the Bible by heart. There is an index which anyone can consult. It is true that the book has tended to weaken the memory, or rather to lessen the task of the memory, but this is surely something for which we ought to be grateful rather than to regret. The book has made that which was difficult to retain easy to possess.

(ii) Socrates' second objection to the book is more serious. It is a twofold objection. First, he objected that you cannot cross-examine a book as you can a teacher. Secondly, he objected that a book cannot defend itself. In a book certain ideas are let loose. It may be that there are people in no state to receive these ideas, people who will actually come to harm because they do not possess the mind, the maturity or the background to assimilate or benefit from these ideas, people whose minds are more likely to be upset than helped by these ideas. Further, these ideas can be misquoted, misunderstood, deliberately twisted and misrepresented, and the book can do nothing about it. Once in the middle of a conversation as a man approached, Dr Johnson said: 'Let us be silent, a fool is coming.' But a book cannot be silent.

The ancient world believed in the voice as a teaching instrument. Papias, that collector of information about the

[handwritten annotation: people no longer need the sermon as a instruction .. books better than most sermons are available in a few cents. So if the sermon cant glow with personality, why not stay home]

early Church, said that he was sure that he would learn more from the living and abiding voice than from any book. It is still quite true that there is a place, and a big place, even in a university, for the transmission of knowledge by the voice to the ear, if for no other reason than that the personality of the teacher can make the subject live as perhaps no book can. It is true that the book can never be the substitute for the voice, but the ideal is when the good book and the voice of the good teacher co-operate together.

(iii) There came a much later objection to the book. Victor Hugo tells of a young French priest holding a printed book in his hand and pointing at a cathedral. 'This', he said, raising the book, 'killed that', pointing to the cathedral. He felt that the printed book had gone far to kill the preached sermon. There is little substance in this objection, for there is one thing that no book can give—the thrill and uplift of worshipping together.

It may be well to remember that there are now certain things which may well prove a threat to the book. At the moment they are only the very thin edge of a very small wedge, no more than a cloud the size of a man's hand on the horizon, but the bookseller would be well advised to know in advance what he is going to do about them. There are emerging the long-playing gramophone records of speech and the tape-recording. They have the great advantage of giving the living voice, and therefore something of the personality of the speaker. A book of 80,000 words can be put on a four-track tape which will play for four hours, and it will cost about twenty-six shillings. This will come. Who is to sell these things? The bookseller or the record shop? It seems to me that the bookseller would be well advised to welcome this development, to lay hold on it in advance, and to get in on it in its earliest stages. It is conceivable that the day will come when this will be as common as printed books.

We have thought about the book; now let us think about

the author. It would be possible to use many different kinds of classifications. An obvious one, for example, would be to divide books into those which are written to entertain and those which are written to instruct, the books which are written for pleasure and the books which are written for study. But there is one distinction which might be popularly made, and which in one sense is true, and which in another sense is false. Nevertheless we begin with this distinction. There are the books which are written by what would popularly be called inspiration, the books which a man writes out of his own free will, the books which he chooses to write, the books which may even be said to be forced out of an author because he cannot help it. And there are the books which are written as a piece of work and craftsmanship, as a professional job, the books which are commissioned, the books which, not to put too fine a point upon it, the writer writes to order.

(i) There is no doubt at all that there are books which are torn out of a man. F. W. Maitland's advice to H. A. L. Fisher was: 'No one should teach philosophy at a university unless he thinks he has it in him to make a system of his own, or is zealous to preach the system of another.' As Maitland saw it, it is necessary to have something entirely personal to give. Quiller Couch said: 'A small man can produce a great book, if he knows how to put almost the whole of himself into it.' John van Druten tells in his autobiography how he took some poems he had written to Sir J. C. Squire for criticism. Squire said that they were too imitative. 'No artist,' Squire said, 'ever produced a genuine work of art, unless he was first sincerely moved by his subject.' Perhaps the most extraordinary example of this was A. E. Housman, the writer of the famous 'Shropshire Lad' poems. He stipulated that there should be no royalties; if there was any profit, it must be used for cheaper editions. He returned American cheques uncashed. He had written, *use,*

he said, because he could not help himself. He would no more think of selling what had been wrung from his heart than he would have cut off his hand and sent it to market. The thing was forced from him. When Carlyle sent the *French Revolution* out into the world, he said of the reviewers, 'Let them say what they like about it. They never had a book that came straighter from the heart of any man.'

Iu
x

Iu
architecture

There is no doubt at all that this kind of book can happen. John R. Allan writing of Lincoln Cathedral says: 'A cathedral, or any church, must be more than a building if it is to mean anything more than temporal glory; it must be a vision of heaven expressed on earth.' So then a book can be a vision of heaven expressed on earth. When that happens, then, as a certain poet said of a man who had the magic of words, 'the words became alive and walked up and down in the hearts of his hearers'. J. S. Whale quotes a passage from Calvin: 'God's word is uttered by men like ourselves; common men who may even be much inferior to us in dignity and social importance. But when some insignificant little man is raised up out of the dust to speak God's word, he is God's own minister.'

Iu

Iu
use.

Unquestionably there are these books with the prophetic accent and when they emerge they have a terrific impact on the world; but when we are discussing the normal day-to-day routine task of communicating the Gospel, they are not very relevant, because we cannot command them; we can only wait for them. No publisher on earth can commission a book like that; he can only pray that he will recognize it when it comes.

(ii) So then we come to the other kind of author, the author who can and will work to order, the author who is a good craftsman, the author who given a job to do does it well.

The strange thing is that this is oddly enough precisely the way in which many of the greatest authors did in fact work. The works which we regard as works of inspiration *on preperation more than inspiration.*

were often the works of sweat and toil. Haydn the great
composer was once asked why he had never written a piano
quintette. His answer was quite simply: 'Because no one
ever ordered one.' In the same realm we can remember the
immortal J. S. Bach turning out his anthems and cantatas
Sunday by Sunday for the choir of St Thomas's Church in
Leipzig to sing, and stacking them in the organ cupboard for
future generations to find and wonder at.

It is one of the oddest facts in literature, as Alasdair Alpine
Macgregor points out, that Tennyson and Byron, two of the
greatest masters of the felicitous rhyme in all literature, made
consistent use of rhyming dictionaries to write their poetry.
There are few more astonishing facts than the fact that
Tennyson's mellifluous melodies and Byron's rhyming can
be traced back to a rhyming dictionary. 'Poems', comments
Mr Macgregor, 'are wrought out, not tossed out.' There is a
description of how John Buchan wrote: 'His daily routine
afforded him six clear hours of work, and he put in that
amount of work every day; much persistence is infinitely
more effective than spasmodic effort however great. Again,
his concentration in work during the time allotted to it was
complete. His morning session, which broke the back of the
day's work, was a really solid four hours' work, unbroken by
any looks at the morning paper, coffees, pauses to light
cigarettes, or any other of the time-wasting expedients of
frail mankind.' Balzac speaks of 'plying the pick for dear
life like an entombed miner'. Flaubert describes himself:
'Sick, irritated, the prey a thousand times a day of cruel
pain', but, 'continuing my labour like a true working-man,
who, with sleeves turned up, in the sweat of his brow, beats
away at his anvil, whether it rain or blow, hail or thunder.'
There is little here of the way in which the public thinks that
an inspired work is produced.

One of the strangest instances of all is that of W. B. Yeats,
the great Irish poet. He writes describing a time spent in the

I

foppery

house of Lady Gregory after an illness: 'I asked her to send me to my work every day at eleven o'clock, and at some other hour to my letters, rating me with idleness, if need be, and I doubt if I should have done much with my life but for her firmness and her care.' It is an extraordinary thing to think of a poet sent to his study at 11 a.m. to write a poem— but it happened. Arnold Bennett had a notice on his mantelpiece: 'Don't waste another man's time.' James Sanderson, the great editor of the *Sunday Pictorial*, was found dead on his bed, with the last sheets of the proofs corrected in his own handwriting.

The idea of waiting for inspiration did not enter the minds of the great writers—they wrote. Johnson said of Gray the poet: 'He had a notion, not very peculiar, that he could not write but at certain times, or at happy moments; a fantastic foppery to which my kindness for a man of learning wishes him to have been superior.' Never was advice given so effectively and so forcefully as it was given by Mr Churchill, as he then was, to Mr Beverley Nichols, as Mr Nichols tells of it in his autobiography *Twenty-five*. Mr Nichols had just written *Prelude*, the work which brought him fame. Mr Churchill asked him how long he had taken to write it. Mr Nichols said it had been written in spasms over five months. Mr Churchill demanded if Mr Nichols did not go to his desk every morning and write. Mr Nichols said that he had to wait for the mood and the inspiration. Mr Churchill answered: 'Nonsense; you should go to your room every morning at 9 o'clock and say, I'm going to write for four hours.' Mr Nichols put forward all kinds of objections—the possibility of toothache, indigestion, inability to get down to it. Mr Churchill answered: 'You've got to get over that. If you sit waiting for inspiration you will sit waiting until you are an old man. Writing is like any other job—like marching an army, for instance. If you sit down and wait till the weather is fine, you won't get far with your troops. Kick yourself; irritate yourself; but *write*; it's the only way.' And Churchill was the unanswerable proof that it could be done.

It was Edison who said that genius is one per cent inspiration and ninety-nine per cent perspiration, and Colin Brooke quotes an American saying: 'The art of writing is the art of applying the seat of the pants to the seat of the chair.'

Herein is precisely the hope for Christian communication. We do not need to find men to write with the divine but unaccountable inspiration; we can find men who will do a craftsman's job, for the harder and the more conscientiously and the more disciplinedly a man works, the more the Holy Spirit will use him.

We have now thought about the book itself and about the author; we must go on to think of the qualities in a book which are necessary, if that book is to communicate its message as widely as possible.

(i) The first quality that is necessary is *clarity*. There was a time when to be obscure was to be great. It is related that an old woman was asked how she had liked the sermon of a once-famous preacher, and that she answered: 'God forbid that I should understand the great man!' But the days when greatness and obscurity were identified are long since past. The first duty of an author is to be clear. H. G. Wells gratefully witnessed to the influence that Huxley had upon him. He said of Huxley's teaching: 'It left me under that urgency for coherence and consistency, that repugnance from haphazard assumptions and arbitrary statements, which is the essential distinction of the educated from the uneducated mind.' Eric Linklater quoted Professor Jack of Aberdeen: 'A writer should remember his manners, and for a writer the best of good manners is clarity. Clarity is also the debt he owes to his readers.' Somerset Maugham summed up his aims as a writer in three words: 'Lucidity; simplicity, euphony', and he quotes with approval Johnson's verdict on Dryden: 'He appeared to have no other art than that of

expressing with clearness what he thought with vigour.'
R. C. Blumenfeld, the great journalist, tells of the advice that
Robert Louis Stevenson gave to him when he was a young
man: 'Never confuse your reader; never take liberties with
your reader's intelligence. . . . Never write without considera-
tion. Think first and write afterwards.'

In good writing there can be, and there ought to be, a kind
of vivid pictorialness with the clarity of an etching, a clarity
which leaves the reader seeing the scene, or mentally seeing
the argument. Humbert Wolfe tells how de Maupassant
learned to write. When de Maupassant was a young man, he
took to Flaubert a story in the course of which he described a
man descending from a cab. 'It is not wholly bad,' said
Flaubert, 'but I do not *see* the man descending, nor yet the
cab.' Three times de Maupassant altered the description
and three times the master made the same criticism. On the
fourth occasion he cried: 'Now I *see* the man and the cab.'
Since then de Maupassant always made the man and the cab
visible and audible, and that is already something. The
writer always needs this vivid, pictorial clarity, and in the
writing of a religious book he needs it more than ever,
because in a religious book, either directly or indirectly, either
by frontal attack or by implication, he will be presenting a
case, and no one will accept a case unless he understands it.

(ii) This leads us to the second necessity, the necessity of
simplicity. Simplicity does not mean either cheapness or
superficiality. Simplicity does not mean that the thing was
done and expressed easily. Depth of thought and simplicity
of expression can go hand in hand, as anyone who has read
the New Testament can clearly see.

There has always been in some places a cult of obscurity.
Johnson, speaking of certain books of his day, said: 'Many
of the books which now crowd the world may justly be
suspected to be written for the sake of some invisible order
of beings—for surely they are no use to any of the corporeal

inhabitants of the world.' Here is the contrast with a preacher and writer like John Wesley. Wesley wrote and spoke the language of the people with a simplicity that they could understand. We note Wesley's protest against the language commonly used in what he calls Bodies of Divinity; it is a protest against theological jargon. It is sometimes argued that just as every science must have its technical jargon, so must religion. The analogy is bad, as I have said above. The other sciences are the spheres of the expert; most of us can get along very well without understanding anything about them. It will not matter greatly to me if I never understand the technical terminology of electricity or automobile engineering or nuclear physics; these things are the field of the expert; I can live well enough without them. But religion is every man's concern, and therefore must be understandable by every man. There may be such a thing as a theological expert; but there is no such thing as a religious expert. It may be that theology is the area of the expert, but religion certainly is not. And therefore there is neither reason nor excuse for using language about religion which cannot be understood.

(iii) We have seen the necessity of clarity and the necessity of simplicity, but there is a third necessity; if the Christian message is to be communicated in print, there is the necessity of *beauty*. We remember Somerset Maugham's three aims— lucidity, simplicity and euphony. In his autobiographical volume, *The Turbulent Years*, Alasdair Alpin Macgregor has an interesting analogy. He quotes Max Beerbohm: 'Form is the goblet for the wine.' Then he goes on to say: 'Be the wine never so good, is not our enjoyment of it diminished, if the hospitable vintner pours it forth for us to be lapped up from the ground with our tongue?' We would not need to go this length. I have always felt that no drink ever tastes so good from a plastic tumbler as it does from glass, and better still from crystal.

Style matters. All cooks use the same ingredients, and yet, out of exactly and precisely the same ingredients, of two cooks one can produce a dish fit to set before a king, the other a stomach-turning mess. Just so, those who speak and write on Christian truth are working with the same facts and the same ideas. What they say will be commended by how they say it; the style can attract or repel. The husk may be so rough and so tough that the kernel is never reached.

At this particular time this needs to be said. Pendulums have a way of swinging and at the moment we are suffering from the swing. Not so very long ago the preacher aimed at being an orator, and the writer wrote a rotund and sonorous style. There has been a complete departure from that and the aim of the preacher has been to become pleasantly conversational and of the writer to be colloquial and almost without style. So far has the pendulum swung that it is difficult now to persuade students to write their sermons at all. Notes—so they think—will do, and—so they plan—they will just talk. Very few people write well nowadays because very few people write at all. There is what almost amounts to a fear of good writing. But to commend the message the message must be well written and spoken. As everyone knows, it is so often the packaging that sells the article and the dust-cover that sells the book. To the clarity and the simplicity with which he would communicate the Christian truth in speech or in print the author must add a certain beauty of style. The fashion of formlessness has gone too far, and too often conversation has become a substitute for proclamation.

(iv) There is still another element which Christian communication must have. It must have clarity; it must have simplicity; it must have a certain beauty; but to that there is still something to be added. James Moffatt said of mid-nineteenth-century religion that it failed to appeal to the intelligence, the imagination and the conscience. The appeal to the intelligence and to the imagination comes through the clarity, the simplicity and the beauty; but if there is to be an appeal to the conscience, Christian communication must have the element of _challenge_. Charles Darwin said of a newspaper editor that he was a great man but 'perhaps he was not easily enough disturbed'. The man who would communicate Christian truth must be disturbed and disturbing. 'I preached what I felt,' said Bunyan, 'what I smartingly did feel.' The man who would communicate Christian truth must feel intensely; he must be disturbed by the human situation, and he must make it his business to disturb others —and no one likes to be disturbed.

The great writers were conscious of this, and they welcomed the criticism and the resentment that their disturbing message produced. H. G. Wells said: 'Refusals to listen and cries of disagreement are not suppression, and it would ill become so advanced a thinker to complain of them; they are recognition.' George Bernard Shaw said: 'If you do not say a thing in an irritating way, you may just as well not say it at all, since nobody will trouble themselves about anything that does not trouble them.' Shaw once said that the biggest compliment you can pay an author is publicly to burn his books, for you have thereby admitted that they are so explosively effective that you want to obliterate them. W. M. Macgregor applies to A. B. Bruce a saying of the good bishop in _Les Misérables_. Bruce was a scholar who awakened New Testament scholarship from its lethargy in Scotland; it was said of him by one of his students: 'He cut the cables and gave us a glimpse of the blue water.' But the saying which Macgregor quotes is: 'I always bothered some of them, for through me the outside air came at them; my presence in their company made them feel as if a door had been left open, and there was a draught.' Even in the most intellectual and philosophic theology there was and must always be this element of challenge, for any theology must aim to provide a knowledge that issues in action.

(v) Now here we have our problem. Christian communication must have clarity, simplicity, beauty and challenge. But the problem is that Christian communication is following a well-worn track; it is saying things which people already know; its task is often to remind rather than to instruct. Its task, as Bertram Pollock saw, is to speak *non nova sed nove*, not new things but old things in a new way. The problem is how to present an old truth in such a way that it becomes a new thrill. There is more than one answer to that, and it is when several of these answers coalesce that writer and material and reader catch fire.

(a) It may well be that for a writer himself an old truth suddenly becomes a new discovery. It is a fact of experience that we only ourselves grasp as much of Christian truth as life compels us to. It can therefore happen that an old truth can become shiningly and vividly true and new to a man all of a sudden. To take an example, the doctrine of life after death may be to a man for long no more than a matter for academic argument. Then death invades his own circle; some one very near and very dear to him dies; and that which was a mere exercise in logical argument suddenly becomes quite literally a matter of life and death. The old can become new.

If it is true that experience of life translates into sudden reality that which has once been theoretical and academic, then there is a sense in which the most helpful books on Christian communication will very probably be written by those who have had experience of life. Once someone asked James Agate, himself a very famous dramatic critic, how to become a dramatic critic. Agate gave him a list of about thirty great dramatists whose work he must study, before he could claim to be a critic at all. But, said the questioner, I shall be about forty before I have studied all that. To which

Agate replied: 'You must be at least forty before your opinions can have any value.' A very young author can write a factual or a critical work with great success; but it is very doubtful if he can write a book which will really help men to meet life, until he himself has lived. The first thing that can remint an old truth is the experience of life, which makes that truth personally true. Balfour once said that perfection consists of the dream of youth executed in maturity.

(*b*) The second thing which can make an old truth new is quite simply the power to express it with precision and with vividness. James Agate once said: 'Good writing . . . is a sense of adventure among words, whereby your description of the oldest thing in the world turns it into a new one.' The one thing which will never communicate Christian truth is the expression of that truth in the time-honoured jargon of conventional religious language. There is nothing more valuable for a religious writer than to have someone looking over his shoulder and saying constantly and even irritatingly —'what do you mean by that?' If a man is going to express religious truth to his own generation he must accept the adventure of putting it into the language of his day.

(*c*) The third thing which can make old truth new is the faculty of really seeing things. Ruskin once said that of every hundred men ninety-nine look at things, but only one sees them. James Agate quotes a passage from Arnold Bennett. 'Every scene, even the commonest, is wonderful, if only one can detach oneself, casting off all memory of use and custom, and behold it (as it were) for the first time, in its right, authentic colours, without making comparisons. The novelist should cherish and burnish the faculty of seeing crudely, simply, artlessly, ignorantly, of seeing like a baby or a lunatic, who lives each moment by itself, and tarnishes the present by no remembrance of the past.'

Just think what it must have meant for the first time to hear

God called Abba, Father. Abba is the word which a little
child uses to his father in the home circle. If you find it in
any secular Hebrew, you translate it 'Daddy'. Just think of
the staggered amazement of the man who heard that for the
first time. It is quite true that if we sit down before the facts
of Christianity like a little child, they will be new to us, and
we will be able to make them new to others.

(d) So far we have seen that the secret of communication
lies in an attitude to truth, an attitude to words and an
attitude to things. But above all the secret of communication
lies in an attitude to people. That attitude is threefold.

First, it is an attitude of interest. We have all known the
kind of person who, when, for instance, he is talking to you
at a reception, is quite clearly looking all over the place for
someone who is more interesting, or more important, or
who has greater snob value. You know that immediately he
spots such a person, he will bid you a quick good-bye. We
have all known the person who just can't be bothered with
people and who takes no great pains to conceal his boredom.
We have even known the person who has a certain contempt
for those who do not reach his own intellectual or social level,
and who makes it obvious that it is so. The great writers
have almost all had an all-embracing humanity. James Agate
wrote in tribute to G. K. Chesterton: 'Unlike some other
thinkers, Chesterton understood his fellow-men; the woes
of a jockey were as familiar to him as the worries of a
judge. . . . Chesterton more than any other man I have ever
known had the common touch. He would give the whole of
his attention to a bootblack. He had about him that bounty
of heart which men call kindness, and which makes the whole
world kin.' Most of us tend to be interested in our own
sphere and in people who have like interests with ourselves.
This is precisely the fault of so many men in the ministry.
They reach a stage when they never talk anything but shop,
and when their interest is bounded not even by the Church

but by the congregation. They are not interested, for instance, in the ordinary man's sports; they regard the playing of games as beneath them. The plays and the pictures and the television programmes that the ordinary man sees are not in their world, and the books that the ordinary man needs and reads are not on their shelves. Such a man cannot communicate to anyone outside his own sphere. He is the captive of his profession.

I remember once reading—I cannot now tell where—of an experience which Leslie Weatherhead had and which he himself related. He arrived early in an unknown town for an engagement. He could find nowhere to pass the time he had to wait except a public-house. He went in and ordered a glass of lemonade. But very soon he was in animated conversation with some of the men who were there. All too soon the conversation had to come to an end, and Dr Weatherhead had to leave for the church which was practically across the road. As he rose to go, one of the men said to him: 'Sir, if the like of you came in here oftener, perhaps the like of us would go in there oftener'—and he pointed to the church across the road.

It is quite certain that the man whose life is bounded by the Church will never be able to communicate with those who are outside the Church. Communication depends on the necessity of an interest which is as wide as humanity.

Secondly, we might put this in another way. No man can communicate unless he can get alongside his fellow-men. Anatole France said of a certain writer: 'He has ink in his veins instead of blood; he has never even looked out of the window.' It is somewhere told of a young clergyman that he was complaining to Mrs Thrale, Dr Johnson's friend and patroness, about the unintelligence and the limited horizon of his parishioners. They had no interest, he said, except in runts, which are young cows. Mrs Thrale said acidly: 'If Johnson had been their parson, he would have learned to talk about runts.' It is impossible to communicate with a man, if we stand above him, or if there is a gap between us and him. 'I sat where they sat', said the prophet Ezekiel. We find William Penn thanking God that he had had the experience of being a slave. I well remember my father putting his hand on my shoulder the evening on which my mother died and saying through his own sorrow: 'You will have a new note in your preaching now'—and it was so, because I had sat where the mourner had sat.

In point of fact this is the very meaning of the incarnation. The incarnation is God coming alongside man, coming into man's very skin, so that he could see with man's eyes, and think with man's mind, and feel with man's heart. There can be no communication except from alongside our fellow men.

Thirdly, we can put this in still another way, the way which has in it the principle and the essence of the whole matter. *There can be no communication without sympathy*. It may well be said that we cannot communicate with a man until we think ourselves into his position, and until we do so quite deliberately. Keats once said that the true poet has no personality; he is like a chameleon, changing himself to match the situation in which he finds himself. Someone once said that if a poet is watching even a game of billiards he becomes the billiard balls. He identifies himself with every person he meets. The man who would communicate must do that, otherwise he will answer the wrong questions and seek to meet the wrong needs, and will in the end be talking to himself and not to his fellow men. To have sympathy is to be compelled to communicate; not to have it, is to make communication impossible. And, be it remembered, this sympathy is not an inborn and inbuilt gift, it is the outcome of deliberate effort.

There still remains two things to be said—and they are the most important of all.

(i) At this present time it is to all intents and purposes true to say that the book is the most important instrument of religious communication that exists, with the possible exception of the television screen. This is so because today there are in this and in every other country millions of people who never go inside a church at all. If these people are to be reached at all, they must be reached through the ministry of print.

But if they are to be reached, they must first of all be respected. What they need, what they desire, and what they will read, is genuine instruction in the Christian faith and in the Bible. They want genuine teaching and genuine exposition. The biggest tragedy in the religious situation just now is the way in which the Church has undervalued its members and undervalued the ordinary man. They do not want, and they will not read, pleasant little moral essays, sermons and books written with the technique of the children's sermon, autobiographical reminiscence by the writer or the preacher. They want genuine instruction. It is the simple fact that by and large the Church has been afraid to introduce the ordinary man to the results of biblical scholarship and the new thought. They have had the feeling that the people will not *agree* stand it. It is in fact what the people are crying out for.

A friend of mine—not a young man, but a man grown old and wise and distinguished in the ministry—told me an experience of his. In his first country parish he preached a sermon which certainly implied that David was not the author of one of the Psalms. On the Monday morning his senior elder sent for him, and my friend went expecting *by Biblical* and even fearing the worst. The old man said to him: *scholarship* 'You implied that David did not write that Psalm.' 'Yes,' said the minister. 'You have good grounds for this?' asked the old man. 'The scholars can produce reasons and evidence for this?' 'Yes,' said the minister, 'I am honestly sure of that.' The old man rose and to the minister's complete astonishment said: 'I thank God for today, for all my life I have longed to be able to believe that there are certain of the Psalms that David never wrote.' It is a small thing, but it is intensely significant. If I may quote my own experience. I have often tried on the air and in books to bring to people the results of modern scholarship so far as I know them. Of course, I have had angry letters calling me a destroyer of the faith and a heretic; but I have had still more letters from seeking men and women saying: 'If this is so, why were we not told this before ? This is what we have been waiting for.'

The Church will never communicate until it is honest, until ministers stop forgetting in the pulpit all that they have learned in the class room, until in courage and in honesty and in sincerity they respect the people to whom they preach and for whom they write, and treat them as thinking adults and not as children who cannot stand the truth. It is time that the message of the Church ceased to be dictated by a very vocal and dwindling minority of obscurant-ists and it is time that the Church had the courage to tell what it knows to be true.

(ii) There is one last thing to be said. The writing and the publishing and the selling of a book today is a great respon-sibility. Through the medium of the printed page a door is opened into the house and home of the community. Adver-tising today is not so much concerned with telling people where a felt need can be satisfied as it is the creating of a need. A book can be printed in vast numbers; it can be sold at a cheap price; an advertising campaign can create in people's minds the feeling that, if they have not read it, they are missing something that they should have. A review in an influential journal, and especially in the Sunday newspapers, can boost a book's sales to very large numbers. It is therefore clear that an instrument for vast good and for vast evil has been put into our hands. A book can exercise a quite incalculable influence on men's minds for good or evil. Will Carleton, the American poet, has a poem which is a warning:

> Boys flying kites haul in their white-winged birds;
> You can't do that way when you're flying words;
> 'Careful with fire', is good advice, we know,
> 'Careful with words', is ten times doubly so.
> Thoughts unexpressed may sometimes fall back dead,
> But God himself can't kill them when they're said.

A book can be a dynamic and an explosive power for good or for evil, and, once it is printed and sold, nothing can stop the dissemination of its ideas.

We are in a situation today in the middle of the twentieth century in which there is laid upon author, publisher and bookseller an unparalleled responsibility for the dissemination and communication of Christian truth, and it may not be an exaggeration to say that the future of the Christian faith depends on how we together face that responsibility.

8

Guidance for the Preacher from the Greek Literary Critics

IN this article we propose to go to certain of the great Greek literary critics to see what guidance and advice they can give to the man whose task it is to speak and to preach the truth. The three works to which we propose to go are *On Literary Composition*, by Dionysius of Halicarnassus; *On Style*, by Demetrius; and *On the Sublime*, by Longinus. Where we quote these authors, quotations are taken from these works, unless it is otherwise started. No one can deal with these authors without being constantly and deeply in debt to the great editions of W. Rhys Roberts. In the case of Dionysius and Demetrius the quotations are made in Professor Roberts's translations; and in the case of Longinus they are from the translation of A. O. Prickard, except when they are independently made.

It is true that there have been English authors who laboured meticulously at their writing. G. M. Trevelyan, for instance, says, 'I have always taken a good deal of pains with the writing of my books, on the average, before the typing stage' (*An Autobiography and other Essays*). And Ben Jonson wrote the famous criticism of Shakespeare, 'I remember the players have often mentioned it as an honour to Shakespeare that, in his writing (whatsoever he penned), he never blotted out a line. My answer hath been, Would he had blotted out a thousand.' But Professor Roberts has pointed out that 'Our British habit of thought leads us to dwell on the spontaneity of literary achievement rather than on its artistic finish . . . and to insist in a one-sided way, that, where genius begins, rules end' (Dionysius of Halicarnassus, *On Literary Composition*, ix). Swinburne said that 'the test of the highest poetry is that it eludes all tests'. And, with this dictum as a text, George Jackson went on to write: 'In other words, if there is poetry of such a kind that you can take it to pieces and put it together again, and tell how it is done, and all about it, then it is not true poetry at all' (*Half-hours in a Library*, 24). The Greeks thought very differently. No doubt Epicurus had said 'writing is no bother at all', a statement which Dionysius caustically remarked was merely meant 'to forestall the charge of gross laziness and stupidity' (3); while Quintilian, the Roman writer on oratory, dismisses Epicurus with the bleak judgement, 'I have no admiration for Epicurus, who runs away from all discipline' (*Instit. Or.*, II, xvii. 15).

But the Greek insisted on wanting to know how it was done. His, as A. O. Prickard wrote, 'was the wonder which says, "I want to know", not the wonder which hears a voice warning him that the ground is holy' (Longinus, *On the Sublime*, xix). Longinus (1) severely criticized his predecessor Cæcilius because in his work *Concerning Sublimity* he had shown by a vast number of instances what the sublime was, whereas the real need was 'that he should tell us by what specific methods the thing may be made our own'. He goes on (2) to say, ' "Genius," says one, "is inbred, not taught; there is one art for the things of genius, to be born with them." All natural effects are spoilt, they think, by technical rules, and become miserable skeletons. I assert that the reverse will prove true on examination.' 'What Demosthenes shows to be true of the common life of men—that of all good things the greatest is good fortune, but a second, not inferior to the first, is good counsel, and that where the latter

is wanting the former is at once cancelled—we may properly
apply to literature; here Nature fills the place of good fortune,
Art of good counsel.' 'The ancients', said Dionysius (5)
'never thought that words, clauses or periods should be
combined at haphazard. They had rules and principles of
their own; and it was by following these that they composed
so well. What these principles were, I shall try to explain.'
It was the conviction of the Greeks that men like Homer and
Demosthenes were not only men of genius, but that they were
also consummate artists in words.

To that end the Greek literary critics were fearless analysts.
They took the work of the masters to pieces and put it
together again, in order that those whom they were teaching
might reproduce that greatness. So Longinus will discuss
and illustrate the problems of words order (22); the use of
prepositions (10); the employment of singulars and plurals
(23, 24); the variations of tenses (25); the use of asyndeton
(19) and of periphrasis (28). So Demetrius will examine and
illustrate the use of hiatus (68); and how discordant letters
may artistically be made to clash together (48). So Dionysius
will spend long on a fascinating discussion of the letters of
the alphabet (14). Even more fascinatingly interesting is
Dionysius' discussion of the effect on composition of the
various metrical feet (17). He takes the twelve basic rhythms
and evaluates them. 'Beautiful words', said Longinus (30),
'are the light of thought.' But they do not just happen; a man
must compose his words with the same care as a craftsman
fits the pieces into an elaborate mosaic.

On care the Greek passionately insisted. 'Speech,' says
Dionysius (3), 'if flung out carelessly at random, at the same
time spoils the value of the thought. . . . A fine thought is of
no avail unless it be clothed in beautiful language.' And he
gives a grim list (4) of authors, who, because they did not
pay attention to style and composition, 'left behind them
volumes which no man can bring himself to read right to the

end', a list in which is included no less an historian than
Polybius. But for all this meticulous care, the Greek insisted
that any suggestion of artificiality must be avoided like the
plague. 'There is considerable charm', wrote Dionysius
(19), 'among efforts of this kind in what is so composed that
it does not seem to be artificially composed at all.' 'Art',
said Longinus (22), 'is perfect just when it seems to be
nature, and nature successful when the art underlies it
unnoticed.' However carefully wrought the writing or the
speaking might be, it was to the Greek a failure unless it
appeared spontaneous. Longinus laid it down (18) that
'Passionate language is more attractive when it seems to be
born of the occasion, rather than deliberately adopted by the
speaker'. Demetrius stresses this particularly in the case of
invective. 'Indignation needs no art. In such invectives the
words should be simple, and, in a manner, impromptu' (27).
'Anxious attention to niceties of smoothness and harmony
does not betoken anger so much as elegant trifling and a
desire to exhibit one's powers' (300). Pretentious and mis-
placed ingenuity is forbidden. Undignified literary faults
Longinus ascribes (5) almost entirely to 'the craving for
intellectual novelties on which, above all else, our own
generation goes wild.' 'Ill-judged ingenuity', said Demetrius
(28), 'in emotional passages is no better than the proverbial
jest at a funeral.' 'To utter a jest ornately is like beautifying
an ape' (165). Trivial subjects and magniloquence can never
go hand in hand. Again and again the Greeks made it clear,
that, however much care they demanded, they had no use for
a lifeless perfection. 'Precision in detail', said Longinus (33),
'comes perilously near littleness. . . . What is great is hazard-
ous by very reason of its greatness.' The writers of genius
scorned the accuracy that lies in every detail (35). 'Though
far removed from flawless perfection yet all rise above the
mortal' (36). The aim is not 'the success of never failing'
(67), but real sublimity. Demetrius (53) held that 'there is

magniloquence

something trivial in excessive nicety', and advocated 'a certain negligence', for instance, in the use of particles. The perfection which is 'faultily faultless, icily regular, splendidly null' was far from Greek ideal. It is indeed Dionysius' complaint about Isocrates (*De Isocrate*, 2) and in his speeches 'the thought is often the slave of rhythmical expression, and truth is sacrificed to elegance'.

It is clear that to the Greek the basis of good writing and good speaking lay in no other magic than the magic of work. The man who would be great was the man who could and would toil terribly. Dionysius (25) tells us how Isocrates spent ten years composing the Panegyric; how Plato, when he was eighty, did not cease 'to comb and curl his dialogues and reshape them in every way'; he speaks of Plato's 'passion for taking pains'; he tells how, after Plato died, amongst his possessions there was found a tablet with the first sentence of the *Republic* ('I went down to Ariston') arranged and re-arranged in every possible word order. At the very end of his treatise, Dionysius (26), set it down that 'no rules contained in rhetorical manuals can suffice to make experts of those who are determined to dispense with study and practice.' 'Nothing', said Sophocles (*Electra*, 945), 'succeeds without toil.' 'God', said Euripides (*Fragment*, 432), 'is the ally of the man who works.' 'Hard work', said Aristophanes (*Ranae*, 1370), 'and good luck go hand in hand.' Plutarch (*Demosthene*, 8) tells how often in the Assembly at Athens, when it might have been expected that Demosthenes would have had some contribution to make to the debates, and when the people were calling upon him by name to speak, he sat silent, unless he had thought the matter out and had prepared himself to speak. There is something salutary here for a generation of preachers which has come to despise meticulous preparation.

The Greeks believed that the great aim of all speaking was to persuade the hearer. 'Persuasion', said the author of the *Rhetorica ad Alexandrum*, 'is the only object of rhetoric.'

Aristotle defined rhetoric (*Rhet.*, i.2) as 'the faculty of discovering all the possible means of persuasion in any subject'. But Longinus had a higher ideal. To him the object of rhetoric is to produce ecstasy. He held that the power to amaze is always stronger than that which seeks to persuade and please (I). 'The soul is raised by true sublimity, it gains a proud step upwards' (7). Real genius in speaking brings 'a sovereign and irresistible force to bear on every hearer' (I). A man can resist persuasion, for the power to resist it lies within himself; but real oratory lifts a man clean out of himself. Dionysius says of himself when he read Demosthenes (*De Demosthene*, 22), 'When I take up one of his speeches, I am entranced and carried hither and thither, stirred now by one emotion, now by another. I feel distrust, anxiety, fear, disdain, hatred, pity, good-will, anger, jealousy. I am agitated by every passion that can sway the human heart.' And he wonders, if he, as a reader, feels like that, what those who heard the speeches from Demosthenes himself must have felt like, as the greatest of all orators 'spoke from the heart and revealed the promptings of his inmost soul'. The Greeks knew that a man can command his intellect but is never really proof against an assault upon his heart.

First and foremost both the Greek and Latin critics demanded *lucidity* and condemned obscurity. Aristotle laid it down that the first essential of a good style is 'to be clear without being mean' (*Poet.*, xxii. I). Demetrius (17) quotes an unknown writer's saying that, 'Clear expression floods with light the hearer's mind'. Dionysius ranked clarity among the 'essential virtues' (*De Thucydide*, 23). He condemned Thucydides because a man would need a university education to understand what he was talking about (*De Thucydide*, 50). Cicero called obscurity *vitium vel maximum* (*Orator*, ix. 30), and demanded as a first essential *sermo dilucidus* (*De Oratore*, III, ix. 38). Quintilian said that those who speak neatly and lucidly can expect but a small reward, *turgid*

for to do so is only to be free from faults, and not to have acquired any special virtue (*Inst. Or.*, VIII. ii. 22). His ideal is that a man should speak, not in such a way that he can be understood, but in such a way that he cannot be misunderstood (*Inst. Or.*, VIII. ii. 24).

Longinus (3) picks out three basic faults which ruin the orator's effect. First, there is *turgidiness*, which is pompous bombast. Second, there is *puerility* or *frigidity*, which is pedantic conceit. Theophrastus, quoted by Demetrius (114), defines frigidity as 'language which transcends the expression appropriate to the thought'. Demetrius himself (237) defines the kindred fault of *aridity* as the kind of writing in which a writer 'describes a great event in trivial terms'. Third, there is *parenthyrsis*, which means a display of passion in the wrong place, which is probably the most embarrassing of all things to listen to.

We may now, almost at random, collect some of the suggestions which the Greek literary critics offer, to enable a speaker to achieve true greatness.

(1) A speaker must choose great subjects and think great thoughts. Longinus (8) laid down as the first essential 'the faculty of grasping great conceptions'. 'What is serviceable, or perhaps necessary, man can procure; what passes his thought wins his wonder' (25). 'The true orator must have no low, ungenerous spirit, for it is not possible that they who think small thoughts, fit for slaves, and practise them in their daily life, should put out anything to deserve wonder and immortality' (9). 'No slave ever became an orator' (44). Demetrius insisted that 'elevation resides in the subject matter' (75). He quotes Nicias, the painter, as saying that a painter's greatness was shown in his choosing a subject of some amplitude; and that just so, 'elevation results from the choice of a great subject' (76). Longinus has an interesting passage in which he lays it down that there is a kind of essential permanence in great oratory. 'Whenever anything

prolixity

is heard frequently by a man of sense and literary experience, which does not dispose his mind to high thoughts nor leave in it material for fresh reflection, beyond what is actually said, while it sinks, if you look carefully at the whole context, and dwindles away, this can never be true sublimity, being preserved so long only as it is heard. That is really great which gives much food for fresh reflection; which is hard, nay impossible, to resist; of which the memory is strong and indelible' (7). The man who chooses a great text is half-way on the road to preaching a great sermon.

(2) A speaker must speak with passion. 'I should feel confidence', said Longinus, 'in maintaining that nothing reaches great eloquence so surely as genuine passion in the right place' (8). A man will not persuade others to believe that which he does not passionately believe himself.

(3) A speaker must express himself with intensity. 'Sublimity', said Longinus (12), 'lies in intensity.' Demetrius (8) uses a vivid simile. 'As a wild beast gathers itself together, as in a coil, to increase its vigour.' In this connexion Longinus (12) has an interesting comparison between Demosthenes and Cicero. Demosthenes is so intense that he is like a lightning flash or a thunderbolt; Cicero, on the other hand, has amplitude, but not intensity, and resembles a slowly spreading forest fire. This intensity comes from two things. First, it comes from compression. Demetrius said (9), 'It is a mark of superior skill to compress much thought in a little space, just as seeds contain potentially entire trees.' 'The very first grace of style is that which results from compression' (107). 'Prolixity paralyses vigour' (241). Demetrius has a very interesting paragraph (222) in which he advises the speaker not to try to say everything. 'All possible points should not be punctiliously and tediously elaborated, but some should be left to the comprehension and inference of the hearer, who, when he perceives what you have omitted, becomes not only your hearer but your

witness, and a very friendly witness too; for he thinks himself intelligent because you have afforded him the means of showing his intelligence. It seems like a slur upon your hearer to tell him everything, as though he were a simpleton.' The writer of the *Rhetorica ad Alexandrum* has a surgical counsel. He says that we will speak with clarity and force if we remove both from our narrative and our words all that is not absolutely necessary, and leave only the things, the removal of which would make the matter obscure. Intensity and economy of words go hand in hand. Second, intensity comes from vividness and 'vividness arises from exact narration, overlooking no detail and cutting out nothing' (Demetrius, 209). Humbert Wolfe in *Upward Anguish* quotes an interesting parallel to this. 'When de Maupassant was a journeyman, he took to Flaubert a story in the course of which he described a man descending from a cab. "It is not wholly bad," said Flaubert, "but I do not *see* the man descending, nor yet the cab." Three times de Maupassant altered the description and three times the master made the same criticism. On the fourth occasion he said, "Now I see the man and the cab". Since then de Maupassant has always made the man and the cab visible.' The orator must enable the hearer to see what he himself sees.

(4) The speaker must be always on the attack. Longinus (12) points out that Demosthenes keeps his sublimest passages for where 'the hearer is to be hard struck'. Demetrius (279) speaks of the cut and thrust of question and answer in a speech. 'The orator forces his hearer into a sort of corner, so that he seems to be brought to task and to have no answer.' Of a sermon preached in Dunbar in 1766, John Wesley said, 'I had a full stroke at their hearts'. The orator and the preacher are out for a verdict, for they are pleading a case which they know to be true, and which it is supremely important to persuade others to accept.

(5) The speaker must be careful in his choice of words.

Dionysius (3) pleads for utter simplicity. He reminds us that Homer and Herodotus, artists in words as they were, use a diction which 'consists, warp and woof, of the most ordinary and the humblest words, such as might have been used off-hand by a farmer, a seaman, an artisan, or anybody else who takes no account of elegant speech'. They used simple words, 'the labels affixed to nature'. Longinus believed, as we have seen, that 'beautiful words are the light of thought' (30), but at the same time he held (31) that 'vulgar idiom is sometimes much more expressive than ornamental language; it is recognized at once as a touch of common life; and what is familiar is on the way to being credible'. Demetrius (77), however, enters the caveat that, 'usual and current words, though clear, are unimpressive and liable to be held cheap'. The aim is that deceptive simplicity which is in all great speaking. A friend of Sir Edward Grey said of him, 'The first time I met Edward Grey and heard his talk I thought he was elementary; but I soon found he was elemental.'

(6) The speaker will remember and study the masters of the past. It is here that Longinus rises to his greatest (14). All the Greek teachers advised imitation and emulation; but Longinus goes further. If we are writing, we must ask, 'How, if need were, Homer would have said the same thing, how Plato or Demosthenes, or, in history, Thucydides would have made it sublime?' Even further, we should ask, 'How would Homer, were he here, have listened to this phrase of mine? Or Demosthenes? How would they have felt at this?' 'Truly great is this competition, where we assume for our own words such a jury, such an audience, and pretend that before judges and witnesses of such heroic build, we undergo a scrutiny of what we write.' In other words a man must write and speak for ever conscious of the unseen cloud of witnesses who compass him about—and that must mean far more to us than ever it could to Longinus.

But in the end the Greeks knew well that real greatness

lies not in technique but in something beyond that. Longinus (9) summed the matter up in an almost untranslatable phrase, 'Sublimity is the note which rings from a great mind', or, as T. R. Glover translated it, 'Sublimity is the echo of a great soul'. And Demetrius (18) quoted an unknown writer, who ended the whole matter by saying, 'True grandeur consists not in saying grand things, but in doing the things said, after saying them.'